EMPOWERING PRODUCTIVITY – BOOK 4

AN EVERYDAY GUIDE
TO
SCRIVENER 3
FOR
WINDOWS

MARY CRAWFORD

An Everyday Guide to Scrivener 3 for Windows
Empowering Productivity – Book 4

Copyright © 2021 by Mary Crawford

Diversity Ink Press
Mary Crawford
www.MaryCrawfordAuthor.com

ISBN: 978-1-945637-60-5 (print)
ASIN: B08ZWYKS6Z

Published March 23, 2021 by
Diversity Ink Press & Mary Crawford
Author may be reached at:
MaryCrawfordAuthor.com

Printed in The United States of America

To Literature and Latte:

I am grateful beyond words that you created such a phenomenal program to help me be a better author. Your efforts have not gone unnoticed.

Contents

Table of Figures

Why Scrivener 3 for Windows?

One of the first challenges any author faces is deciding where to write their words. Most authors have their favorite program and often defend their choices passionately. I am no exception. I make no bones about the fact that I adore Scrivener. In fact, I own Scrivener for three platforms. It is simply the most comprehensive writing program I have ever encountered.

Scrivener has changed the way I write. It allows me to manage my manuscript, research materials, audio clips, websites and virtually anything else in one spot. Not only does Scrivener allow me to be more efficient as an author, it has made my books more cohesive with fewer errors. I format all my clean and wholesome romances with Scrivener, and the results are beautiful and professional. I'm excited to share the knowledge I've gained over the years to make Scrivener 3 for Windows understandable so it becomes your favorite tool too.

You may have heard that Scrivener is difficult to use and requires a steep learning curve. The purpose of *An Everyday Guide to Scrivener 3 for Windows* is to help demystify the program and show you how it can help you become a stronger writer.

Speaking frankly, until now the Windows version has been a pale version of its Mac counterpart. However, this new upgrade to what was already a very solid program narrows the gap between the two programs substantially.

You don't have to take my word for it. Literature and Latte (the makers of Scrivener and Scapple) offer a thirty-day free trial of the software for you to evaluate. This is not a stripped-down version that lacks features. They allow you to test the program as if you have paid for the application in full. The trial is for thirty days of use. The days don't need to be consecutive. If you use the software every other day, it will last a couple of months. I wouldn't be surprised if you are impressed by improvements in Scrivener 3 for Windows and adopt it as part of your writing process.

If you find the prospect of using Scrivener 3 for Windows daunting or if you are overwhelmed by the new options within the program, this book is for you. My hope is that I can help you become as comfortable with Scrivener as you are the traditional word processing program you grew up using. I'll take you step-by-step through the features of Scrivener 3 for Windows and give you tips on how to make the program work for you.

My Personal Success Story

Those of you who follow me on social media or the writing communities I'm part of might already know I accidentally became an author. It's completely true, I never set out to be an author. In fact, if you had told me that I would grow up to write books for a living, I would've laughed at you. You see, in the seventh grade I had an English teacher who told me I was the worst student he ever had the displeasure of teaching. For decades, I thought his opinion was the gospel truth. Fortunately, I had a chance meeting with an author who encouraged me to expand my horizons and write.

I went to law school and became a civil rights attorney. Unfortunately, health concerns made it difficult for me to work. So, I turned to my first love—reading. I read a book which featured a character with cerebral palsy. I was so excited to read a realistic portrayal of a person with my disability, I wrote to Linda Kage and asked her if she would give this secondary character her own book.

I had never written a fan letter before, so I wasn't expecting much. However, Linda wrote back to me personally and I became her beta reader. Eventually, Linda encouraged me to write my own material. I decided to give it a shot since I could no longer work. In November 2013, I started writing *Until the Stars Fall from the Sky*. By June 2014, it was picked up by a publisher and published. That was thirty-four books ago. Linda had no idea what a prolific writing monster she would create.

Initially, I started writing in Microsoft Word. However, I found it incredibly frustrating to organize my manuscript and to keep all of the supporting documentation together. I tried using a traditional notebook, but it was never as updated as I needed it to be. For example, I would bookmark different sites I was using for reference, yet when I went back to find them, they often were buried.

Fortunately, a fellow author came to my rescue and introduced me to NaNoWriMo. As part of that, I learned about Scrivener. At the time, I was using a Windows computer, so I learned to use Scrivener for Windows before I moved over to a Mac.

Even though Scrivener was more difficult to use with voice recognition software, it was still a boon to my writing. I kept reading all about how difficult the program was to learn. I was a little baffled because I didn't find it all that hard to understand. Aside from my difficulties using Dragon NaturallySpeaking with Scrivener, even though many people warned me Scrivener was impossibly complex and difficult to learn, I found it much more intuitive than I was led to believe. I am a huge fan of Scrivener because it makes organizing my work a breeze.

Then, my computer had a massive meltdown and I had to replace it. Since Scrivener was my favorite writing program and the Mac version had more features than the Windows version, I switched platforms. This enabled me to dictate directly into Scrivener without having to copy and paste. I spend the majority of my time using my MacBook Pro. However, for this book, I am using Scrivener 3 for Windows via Parallels.

I have great news! Most of the disparity between the functionality of the Mac software and the Windows version have been taken care of in Scrivener 3. The upgrade of Scrivener 3 for Windows is much more like its Mac counterpart. It has many of the features I love in the Mac version.

Unfortunately for me, the one thing that hasn't changed is the fact that for those of us who dictate, Scrivener 3 for Windows does not yet offer full text control like Microsoft Word. Therefore, I am dictating into an application called Speech Productivity Pro and copying and pasting my work back into Scrivener. Most of you won't have the same issues as me. Just in case you do, I thought I would share my workaround with you.

Key Features of Scrivener 3

The recurring refrain when people refer to Scrivener for Windows is that it has a steep learning curve. I think this reputation is somewhat undeserved. Many people don't understand that Scrivener changes the paradigm of writing software.

It is different from other word processing programs because it has so many other features. Once you understand how these features interrelate, Scrivener isn't really more difficult than other computer programs you are not familiar with. The great thing about Scrivener is that you don't need to know how to do everything all at once to be able to enjoy the program.

Scrivener 3 for Windows solves a multitude of problems for authors.

You like to work with sticky notes and index cards? No problem. Scrivener has you covered.

Prefer to work with a detailed outline? You can do that too.

You need to keep your research in one place? Scrivener is ideal for that. You can keep websites, audio clips, video clips, extra resource documents, a story bible and virtually anything else you want in your research folder.

Need to track unusual things like the revelation of a big secret, time or location or even characteristics of your characters? Not a problem in Scrivener 3 for Windows. You can use custom metadata, labels and status settings.

If you're in the middle of a project and want to make the switch to Scrivener 3, the program has tools to make that easy.

Do you need help with naming your characters, identifying overused words, or making your manuscript as clean as possible? Scrivener has you covered.

New features in Scrivener 3 for Windows make what was a great program even better. You can still organize your manuscript in the binder and collect your resource material in your research file and compile your documents the way you need them to appear. The compile function has been completely updated to include styles. So, it's easy to format your book as you go along. The compile feature is now much more intuitive as you can see what your output will be. You can customize your formats any way you like. The new version is quite flexible.

There have been upgrades to the way you move around your document as well. In my opinion, the new quick search feature is worth the price of the upgrade. It allows you to search for words in your document and returns the results in context so it's easy to figure out which instance of a word you wish to work with.

One of my favorite parts of this upgrade is the introduction of dark mode. As a migraine sufferer, I used to create my own dark mode by manually changing each color. Now, it is easy to switch to dark mode with a couple of clicks.

The other substantial improvement is the introduction of page view. I know it seems silly, but I like to see my documents as they might appear. Of course, because of the way I have my documents set up, all the fancy chapter headings and section breaks will be added during the compile process. Even so, page view gives me a rough idea of how much progress I am making.

Speaking of progress, it is really easy to track your progress on the new quick search bar. In my opinion, the quick search bar is enough to warrant an upgrade to Scrivener 3 for Windows.

There have been so many upgrades in Scrivener 3, it is impossible for me to talk about them all here. So, I will discuss them individually.

Along the way, I will provide helpful tips. They will be categorized as follows:

Features tips related directly to a specific feature in Scrivener 3 for Windows.

 General tips designed to help you become a Scrivener 3 power user.

 Cautions against potential pitfalls or problems.

 Helpful notes to highlight information.

Additionally, I will be referring to keyboard shortcuts throughout *An Everyday Guide to Scrivener 3 For Windows.* There are not as many keyboard shortcuts listed in the menus as there are in the Mac version. However, the ones that are there can be very helpful.

Most of these are pretty standard Windows vernacular.

 CTRL+X, CTRL+Y simply means hold down the CTRL key then typing XY.

KEYBOARD SHORTCUTS:

- ALT = Alt Key
- WK or Meta = Windows Key
- CTRL = Control Key
- ⌦ = Delete Key
- ↓ = Down Arrow Key
- ↵ = Return Key
- ← = Left Arrow Key
- → = Right Arrow Key
- ⇧ = Shift Key
- ⇥ = Tab Key
- ↑ = Up Arrow Key

Additionally, the icons in your toolbar, which you can customize, also contain tooltips which identify each icon.

While I'm discussing keyboard shortcuts and other computer technology, is a good time for me to remind you that I am not a computer programmer. I am a former lawyer who once was a social worker with a degree in psychology and a doctorate degree in jurisprudence. I am not exceptionally computer savvy. Consequently, this won't be a complete treatise on Scrivener for Windows nor will it be a computer programming guide.

My entire Empowering Productivity series is centered around one author sharing my experience with other authors to make the process of writing easier. *An Everyday Guide to Scrivener 3 for Windows* will focus on the features I use most often in publishing. I hope to help you understand Scrivener 3 for Windows so that it becomes usable software and a powerful tool in your writing arsenal.

Organizing a book for a piece of software as all-encompassing as Scrivener 3 for Windows is its own special challenge. Many of the features are so interrelated that I may need to speak about one feature before I describe another. So, if you are confused, feel free to jump around in the table of contents.

Let's start our journey through Scrivener 3 for Windows by identifying the moving parts.

CHAPTER 2

The Moving Parts

'm not going to pull any punches. Scrivener 3 for Windows can appear very complex. It is a powerful, wide-ranging software program that's probably unlike anything you've ever used before. Even if you have used Scrivener in the past, there are significant improvements in Scrivener 3 for Windows that changed the user interface. Sometimes, this change is minor, other times—like with section layout or styles, the change can seem dramatic.

Before I address individual parts of Scrivener, let me give an overview which might help you better understand how Scrivener works. When new users encounter Scrivener for the first time, they are often overwhelmed by the sheer number of options. This confusion is often compounded by the fact that there are several ways to accomplish the same thing in Scrivener. You can customize your workflow based on your preferences. Many things you can accomplish in Scrivener can be done multiple ways.

I think it helps to view Scrivener as a collection of different software programs instead of one program. I'm showing my age here, but I like to equate Scrivener to a Trapper Keeper. When

I was in school, these were the latest greatest organizational tools on the planet. The Trapper Keeper was far more than just a three-ring binder. It came with a seemingly endless supply of cool accessories. There were special pockets designed to hold papers, pencils, calculators, photographs and business cards. There was even a special ruler with a calculator built in. It was a one stop shop for everything you needed for school. I especially appreciated the fact that you could zip everything inside and latch it closed. I even owned a model with a handle.

So, why am I reminiscing about a binder? Not only were Trapper Keepers a very handy invention for organizing all things school, they make a good analogy to describe what Scrivener can do for your writing process.

Scrivener is far more than just a word processor. The research section in the Binder can be used as a virtual file cabinet. Much like the Trapper Keeper, you can put anything you want in the research section. The other huge benefit of Scrivener is its ability to compile into different formats. You don't need an outside program to create EPUB, DOCX, RTF, PDF or many other types of document formats. It is the consummate document converter.

As you can see, Scrivener has many moving parts which create a comprehensive tool for authors. The first step is to start a project. So, let's start with the project templates, the framework upon which you build your Scrivener project.

Project Templates

When you see a shortcut written out like CTRL G, CTRL N, it simply means to press down the control key at the same time you press G and then N.

The first thing you'll need to do when you open Scrivener is to choose a project template and save your first project (CTRL+G, CTRL+N). In Scrivener, the collection of files, research and formatting options is called a project. They are identified with .scriv.

Scrivener 3 for Windows comes pre-populated with several templates to handle many types of projects. To begin, choose a template which describes the type of document you want to create.

Don't worry too much if you can't find the perfect template or if you are unsure which one to use. You can always add files or documents to your binder later.

For example, if you have chosen to use a blank template and you decide you want the character and place sheets included in your work in progress, you can open a new project using the template you want and simply drag the files over to the document you are working on.

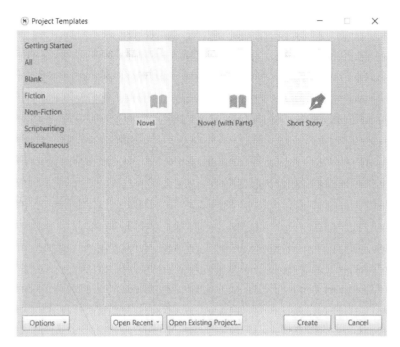

FIGURE 1: Choosing a Template in Scrivener 3 For Windows

Choosing a Template

The first thing Scrivener will do is ask you to name your project and choose a location in which to save it. Where you save it is a matter of personal preference. Since I use the IOS version in addition to Windows, I save my projects to a very specific location to allow the IOS version to find it. So, my path looks like this:

Dropbox ▸ apps ▸ Scrivener ▸ [project name]

This is the default save location in the IOS version.

Regardless of whether you save your projects to the cloud or on your local hard drive, make sure the save function has completed before you exit Scrivener. This is critically important. Failure to do so will result in lost data.

Large files can take a while to save. Please be patient.

Scrivener 3 for Windows has a couple of handy features to help you keep track of your Scrivener project.

First, if you want to find the location of where you last saved your project, you can click on File ▸ Reveal Project Folder. Additionally, if you have saved any themes, preferences or styles, you can find them by choosing File ▸ Reveal Application Support Folder.

Scrivener 3 for Windows has made it easy for you to find projects you work on frequently. You can add any project to the Favorite Projects menu by clicking on File ▸ Add Project to Favorites. Unlike recent projects, this list does not change as you open and close files and the projects are sorted alphabetically to make them easy to find. Any time you want to remove a project from the favorites menu, it is as easy as clicking on Remove Project From Favorites.

When I get a new story idea, in order to avoid bright and shiny syndrome, I start a new Scrivener file and write down my idea and a working title. This enables me to focus on my work-in-progress while I preserve my great idea.

Regardless of which template you use, your project is fully customizable. So, just pick the project which is closest to what you are working on. Scrivener will ask you to name the project after you click on the appropriate template.

Don't get too hung up on which template you choose. If you decide you need to have other options available in another template, you can easily combine them. Simply open a new blank project using any template you want, and choose your favorite folders provided in the template you use and drag them into your work-in-progress.

If you don't find a template to your liking, there are many available online for download. Make sure you unzip the file before trying to import a template.

 If you want to change the name of your project after you created it, the easiest way to do this is to close your file in Scrivener and rename it in Windows Explorer using the rename function.

A Note About Templates

Scrivener comes with a variety of templates by default. However, sometimes you may want to add your own. There are templates for different story beats and plot structures available on the Internet. When you are downloading a template, make sure you unzip the file and run it through a virus check. It is easy to import new templates.

To import a template, choose New Project from the file menu or press CTRL G+ CTRL N. Click on the Options button in the lower left-hand corner and choose Import Template from the drop-down menu.

In order to be imported as a template, the file must be a .scrivtemplate file. If you are moving from Scrivener 1, they will be converted to be compatible with Scrivener 3. For ease of use, you may want to re-save them as Scrivener 3 templates.

You can also choose to save a current project as a template. However, be aware that your file structure needs to be just the bare bones. Otherwise, it will be too large to save as a template.

Such is the case with the "template" I use for my romance novels. If I try to save it as a template, Scrivener warns me that it is too large. Therefore, I have made a blank novel template from a project.

When I create a new project for a romance novel, I open my Mary's Blank Novel project and use the Save As feature. I give the project a new name. Then, in the new work-in-progress, I use the Project Replace function to change my character names. If you choose to take this approach, make sure you change the title of your project in the metadata. Because I often work with several files at once, I take care to change the color of the character labels so I can tell which novel I am working on at a glance.

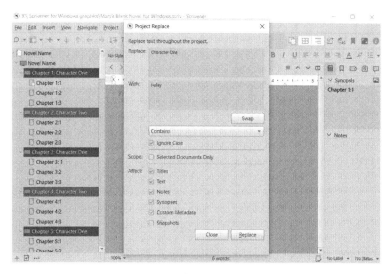

FIGURE 2: Using Project Search and Replace to Customize a Project Used as a Template

Typically, I don't recommend using the Save As command to routinely save your work. For some reason, using the Save As command tends to confuse Scrivener and result in data loss. This is especially true if you use a cloud service like Dropbox.

However, I do use the Save As command so that I can use a stripped-down project which is too big to be saved in the templates folder as an actual template. My Blank Novel project is too big to be saved as an official template because I include information such as story beats and character sheets. You may not need to use my work-around, but in case you do, I thought I would share.

If your file is small enough that you can use the Save As Template command under File, your template will be available on the list of templates when you start a new project. Any templates you import will also show on the list of templates. When you import a new template, you will be able to choose the category in which it appears.

If your templates are smaller than mine, you can use the Save As Template command on the File menu. If you are able to do it this way, your custom template will appear when you set up a new file.

There are templates available on the Internet that can be imported into your Scrivener program. Use these with caution and virus check them first. Some of these files will cut down on your set up time. One of my favorites is *Romancing the Beat* by Gwen Haynes. Her template is available for free on her Internet site. If romance is not your thing, there are several others available for the Snowflake Method, Save the Cat, and A Hero's Journey.

It's actually quite easy to import templates into Scrivener 3.

- Open a new project.
- Click on Options in the lower left-hand corner.
- Click on import template.
- Choose the template file from wherever you saved it.
- You will be given the opportunity to categorize your template.
- Your new template should now appear in whichever category you placed it in.

For example, I have imported a Snowflake Method template as well as a *Romancing the Beat* template. Although these templates can be helpful, if you wish, you can build your own novel by starting with a completely blank template.

Once you have chosen a template, now it's time to work with your project. To do this, it's helpful to know about the working parts of Scrivener 3.

First, I'm going to talk about the footer status bar. I will refer to other key parts of Scrivener while I discuss the footer status bar, but don't worry I will fully explain each part later. The Header and Footer Status Bar are very valuable tools for working with your manuscript.

Where to Save Your File

If you are using Scrivener on different computers, you may want to use a cloud-based storage location in which to save your file. If you plan to use your project with the iOS version of Scrivener, you will need access to Dropbox.

 Although you can use other cloud services to save your backup copies in Scrivener 3 for Windows, I don't recommend using them as your primary save location because they often include conversion software which messes with Scrivener.

Even though I don't use the IOS version a lot, I still save all my projects in the Scrivener file in my apps folder on Dropbox. There is a downside to this approach though. The IOS version requires lots of time to sync your files. So, if you have lots of files in this folder, it could take a substantial amount of time before they are ready to use on your mobile device. If this is an issue, just move the Scrivener files you are not actively using to a different location.

Now that we discussed choosing a template for your project and where to save it, I'm going to talk about the Header Status Bar and the Footer Status Bar and how they help you work with your project.

The Header Status Bar

Right below the formatting bar, is a very helpful toolbar which is really easy to overlook. However, it is quite powerful. I call it the Header Status Bar. This is a toolbar which changes its content depending upon which editing window you are in.

FIGURE 3: Header Status Bar in Scrivener 3

For example, if you are using the Scrivenings mode, it contains the name of the folder you are currently using. If you hover your mouse over the top of this title, the whole path will be displayed. The first two arrows on the right-hand side enable you to move between the last document you worked on and your current one.

On the right-hand side is an icon with three bars. If you click on that icon, it will show you the structure of your document (if it has sub-folders). This feature is particularly handy if you are working with a complex document with many levels in the Binder.

The up and down arrows move you between the documents in your section. Note that these features work in the chapter and scene levels. The top folder, frequently called Draft or Manuscript, does not display the same information.

Lastly, there is a toggle switch for splitting your screen. You can split your screen vertically or horizontally. In Figure 4, I have split my window to show one editor in Outline Mode and the other in Scrivenings mode.

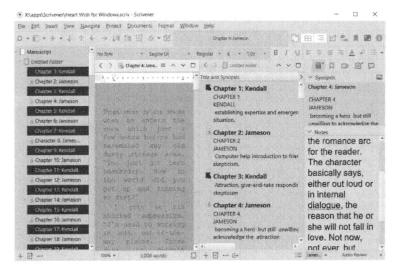

FIGURE 4: Split Window Containing Binder, Scrivenings , Outlining Mode, and the Inspector

If you click on View ▸ Editor Layout you can change the orientation of your split panes from horizontal to vertical. When you are finished operating in split windows, just click on the icon again and you will go back to one window.

When you are in split screen mode, the active window always has a blue status bar at the top of the window.

The color change at the top of the window enables you to tell which window is active. I know this seems self-evident, but when you have several windows open, it can sometimes get confusing.

If you have your editing panes in different modes, make sure to choose which editing mode you want to be in before toggling back to one window.

If you find yourself using the editing windows in Scrivener in a particular pattern that suits you, you can save your layout with the Window ▸ Layouts ▸ Manage Layouts menu command. To save your custom layout, choose the + sign and give your layout a unique name. Scrivener 3 will take a snapshot of the layout and give you an opportunity to use the current layout. You can also choose to save your corkboard and outliner preferences and your metadata if you wish. For example, I have a view I like to use when I have my large monitor and a different arrangement when I'm just using my laptop and monitor space is at a premium. If you want to switch layouts, just go to Window ▸ Layouts ▸ Manage Layouts and choose the saved layout you would like to use. Additionally, by clicking on the ellipsis, you have the option to import and export layouts.

The counterpart to the Header Status Bar is another dynamic toolbar I refer to as the Footer Status Bar.

The Footer Status Bar

At the bottom of any Scrivener project, there is a dynamic Footer Status Bar. Its contents change based on which mode you are operating in. it is one of the most quietly powerful features in Scrivener. It's not flashy, but it contains many helpful settings.

The footer bar appears at the bottom of your window. In the following figure, I broke it down to four different parts, but on your computer, it will appear as one long bar across the bottom of your Scrivener window. The footer status bar can show a variety of things, including your word count (if you are operating in Scrivenings mode). The options change depending on which mode you are in.

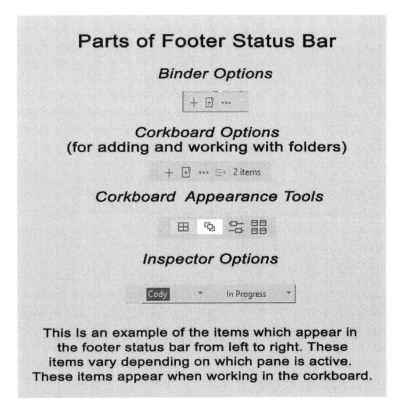

FIGURE 5: Parts of Footer Status Bar

If you are working in the Scrivenings mode, you will see a target which allows you to set goals for each individual folder or document in your binder. Additionally, there is a piece of paper. If you check that box, the document will appear in the compiler. If you have written yourself notes to help your storyline stay on track and used the binder to store the information, you may want to use this option to uncheck the piece of paper, so it doesn't end up in your final product.

Binder Options

On the right-hand side of the Footer Status Bar, you'll find options for your Binder. You can add documents by clicking the + or add a folder by clicking on the folder with the + sign.

Clicking on the ellipsis (…) will bring up another menu. From this menu, you are able to do many things. The options in this menu can change depending on your template. For example, if you are writing a fiction novel, there might be options to add character or setting sheets.

One of the most helpful features is the ability to duplicate existing folders. The keyboard shortcut for this feature is CTRL D. This will duplicate your folders or documents. The new folder or document name will have the word copy behind it. To duplicate your file without its subfiles, you can press CTRL ⇧D.

You can also add folders to the trash from this menu or assign a section, label, or status designation. This menu will also allow you to move or copy folders.

We'll talk about collections later in Chapter 6, but among other things, this is a particularly powerful tool for checking for consistency within your manuscript.

If you want to change your document to a folder or your folder to a document, you can do so from this menu. From a practical standpoint, there is very little difference between a document and a folder in Scrivener 3. I prefer to work in folders because Scrivener 3 will show you the sub-folders if you click on the parent folder. If you do the same in a document, the sub-documents will not be shown. Additionally, the default separators are different in files and documents. This can negatively affect your automatically generated table of contents—unless you adjust the properties in Compile.

Bookmarks are a new feature in Scrivener 3, and you can add them by right clicking on the Binder. I will talk about bookmarks under the Inspector section of this chapter.

If you prefer to work in a language other than English, you can choose for Scrivener to display a different language under File ▸ Options ▸ General ▸ Language.

Corkboard Options

When working in Corkboard Mode, the next section of the Footer Status Bar looks very similar to what you just saw in the Binder options. However, these icons control the corkboard window. So, you can add new documents or folders.

If you click on the ellipsis, there will be a variety of options similar to the ones available in the Binder option. You can add and delete documents (in this view, they appear as index cards) or move them to the trash. From this menu, you can also move or copy folders.

The icon to the right of the gear is grayed out unless you're working in Corkboard Mode with another window open (such as split screen or if the copy holder is open). To use this tool, make sure your split screen or copy holder is open and then click on the folder you want to open in the other window. It defaults to whatever group mode you have selected for the split screen.

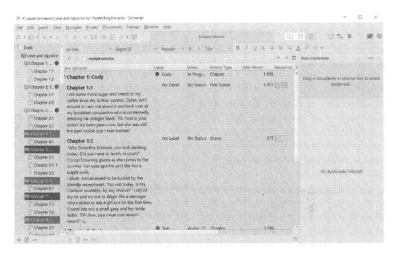

FIGURE 6: Automatic Selection Tool in Split Screen

Honestly, before writing this book, I had never used that function before. I'm glad I discovered it because it solved one of the frustrations I have with using the corkboard. Sometimes, I want to see the sub-folders at the same time I look at the overall structure of my document. This tool allows that to happen.

Corkboard Appearance

The next section on the Footer Status Bar is an area in which you can change the appearance of your corkboard. You can line up your index cards several ways and customize the size of the card and how many appear in a row. Scrivener has two main modes in the corkboard. One is a traditional view of your corkboard. The other allows you to move your files free-form and only commit them to your Binder when you choose. This is handy if you're moving around scenes and you're not exactly sure where you want them to go.

The last option is Arrange by Label. You can arrange your index cards to be presented vertically or horizontally. This feature is helpful if you are trying to track a particular point of view, timeline or location. You can toggle back and forth between the Arrange By Label or the traditional view.

 Scrivener now uses a pale "cork" color instead of a real-world texture, but if you prefer the old school look, you can find it in the Corkboard background setting under Options ▸ Appearance ▸ Corkboard settings

One neat way to customize your index cards is to change the icon. Scrivener comes with many options; however, you can also import your own custom icons into Scrivener. To do this, right-click on the folder in one of your index cards. Then, choose Change Icon and a menu will appear. At the very top of the menu is an option to Manage Custom Icons. There are many places where you can download icons for free or purchase a selection of them. Additionally, there are some available on the Literature and Latte site in this thread.

https://www.literatureandlatte.com/forum/viewtopic.php?f=18&t=17688

Inspector Options

In the Inspector options, you can change the label type as well as the status.

Changing these options in the Inspector will change them in your Binder, Corkboard Mode and Outline Mode.

When you click on label, you are presented with a list of labels which already exist in your project. If you want to add or change options, scroll down to the bottom of this list to edit. You can edit both the label title and the color. Sometimes, if I am labeling to mark consistency, I assign one-character various shades of labels in a single color to help me visually track things.

The status options come pre-populated with some common choices like to-do, first draft, second draft, final draft, etc. However, you can add whatever you wish by clicking on edit. For example, I use a grammar checking program called ProWritingAid. So, after I run a chapter or section through the software program, I mark it as PWA cleared. After I listen to a chapter or scene (using the audio read back feature in the Windows operating system), I change the status to audio cleared. You can continue to change the status of your folders throughout the progress of writing your manuscript. However, if you use labels in your compile process, make sure you change them back to the original settings before you compile.

Speaking from personal experience, there is nothing more satisfying than being able to change the status to **done**.

Binder

The binder is the backbone of your Scrivener project. It is likely already displayed when you open your project. However, if it is not, you can open it with the menu by going to View ▸ Binder or by pressing CTRL ⇧ B. Additionally you can click on the blue view button on your toolbar and check Binder.

 If you click on the triangle icon beside the folder or document, it will expand sub-folders or sub-documents, if there are any. If you want to use a keyboard shortcut, click on the top level of the folder or document in the binder you wish to examine and use CTRL with the arrow keys. This works to move your folders or documents up and down your binder. This will also allow you to change the hierarchy of a folder.

Files and documents are arranged in a hierarchical fashion. This may become important later when you format your work. In my opinion, the easiest way to move files or documents in your binder is to add the arrow keys to your toolbar. I will discuss customizing your Toolbar in more detail in Chapter 3. However, you can also move items in your binder by clicking and dragging them. A blue bar will appear where the files or files will be inserted based on where you drag it. Alternatively, you can right-click on any folder or document in your binder and choose Move To from the menu.

Mandatory Files

The Binder acts like a three-ring notebook. Although you can add files and documents to the binder easily, there are three mandatory files in the binder. The mandatory files are the Draft Folder, Research Folder and the Trash Folder. I will discuss each in a little more detail.

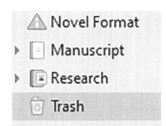

FIGURE 7: Mandatory File Types in Scrivener 3 For Windows

The Draft Folder is where your manuscript is kept. The only exception to this is your front and back matter. In the following example, the Draft Folder is referred to as Manuscript. Depending upon the template you used to create your project, this folder may be called manuscript, screenplay or novel. You can change the name of this folder, but you cannot delete it.

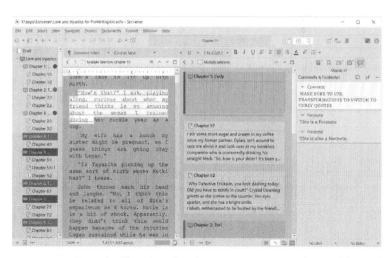

FIGURE 8: Sample Showing Binder, Document Mode, Corkboard Mode and Inspector

As you can see from Figure 8, I write my novels in chapters and scenes. I label each scene (even though it doesn't appear that way in my table of contents) to make it easier to locate text in the Quick Search feature. My editor windows are shown in split screen. In one half, I have Document Mode displayed while I am showing my Corkboard in the other window. Additionally, my inspector is shown with a bookmark.

The Research Folder is where everything else goes, including your front and back matter, because they are treated differently during the compile process. There really is almost no limit to what you can place in the Research Folder. I use it to keep a copy of my e-book cover, any graphics I use in my chapter headings and section breaks, as well as websites I use for reference. You can even save movie and audio clips here. With the exception of your front and back matter folders, what is in this Research Folder is not included when you compile your documents for publication.

The Trash Folder is exactly what it sounds like. It is where you place things you no longer want. Files stay in the trash until you empty the trash.

Draft Folder

For purposes of simplicity, I will refer to the first mandatory type of file as a Draft Folder. However, the name for this folder may vary depending upon the type of template you started with. It can also be referred to as manuscript, screenplay or novel. You can change the name of this folder, but you cannot delete it.

The Draft Folder is where you keep your manuscript. You can add and subtract files and documents. How you structure your files or documents in the Draft Folder is entirely up to you. Some authors prefer to write their novels as one block of text and divide it into chapters and scenes later. Others, like me, separate their scenes as they write. Some authors treat the binder like an elaborate outline with several levels of hierarchy within the binder. Scrivener is adaptable to any writing style.

Either style of writing works well with Scrivener 3 for Windows. If you want to write your text in one big block and divide it into chapters later, Scrivener has tools to help with this.

Additionally, if you are a person who likes to see your scenes broken down into many different levels, Scrivener can accommodate this style of writing as well.

In the following example, I added eight levels in the binder. I could've continued to add more, but it would've been redundant.

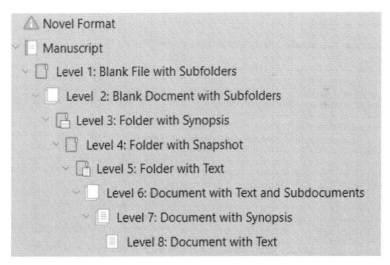

FIGURE 9: Levels in Binder Showing Different Icons Indicating Content in Scrivener 3 for Windows

You will see from the illustration that Scrivener 3 for Windows uses different icons depending upon the content of each folder. Unlike the Mac version of Scrivener 3, the icon containing the snapshot did not change. (Although, like the Mac version, in the Inspector there is a dot beside the camera icon).

The different icons for each type of content are helpful if you jump around in your manuscript. This feature is one of the most liberating in all of Scrivener. You are no longer restricted to writing in a lineal fashion. If the inspiration strikes to write a different portion of your story, you can simply go to that folder or document in your binder and start writing. Labels, comments and status settings can help you keep track of your progress.

You may add as many folders and documents to this folder as you want. However, items in the draft folder must only contain text. You can insert pictures into files in the draft folder, but you can't drag them directly into it. Folders and documents in your draft folder have a hierarchy much like an outline. This hierarchy becomes important when you apply formatting.

In Scrivener 3 for Windows, there is a new function called Section Type. This will come into play when you compile your document. You can right-click any folder or document in your binder and apply a section type, label or status. We will discuss all of these things in Chapter 5.

Research Folder

You need to add pictures for your chapter headings or graphics used for scene dividers to the research folder.

The Research Folder is used to collect everything that is not your manuscript. Your front and back matter go into the research folder because they are treated differently during the compile process. Putting them in the Research Folder ensures that they have the proper page numbering separate from the rest of your manuscript.

The Research Folder can be used to store almost anything. This includes websites, audio clips, video clips, pictures and files containing notes which you don't want to appear in your manuscript.

Additionally, any images you use in your document as scene separators are stored in this file. If you are compiling to an e-book and you wish to have a cover attached, you would place your cover file here. The easiest way to add image files to your research folder is to drag them in from Windows Explorer.

You can drag websites into your Research Folder. To do this, make sure both windows are minimized. If you are having trouble keeping your Scrivener project visible, click on Window ▸ Bring All to Front. Dragging websites into your Draft Folder will not work. They need to be in your Research Folder.

 Links added to the research section are computer specific. If you use your project on several computers, and you are linking to documents, they need to be present on each computer. One solution is to put your linked documents on the cloud.

I also like to keep pictures of locations and characters in my Research Folder. This allows me to give consistent descriptions throughout each novel and series. If you have a series bible, it would also go in that Research Folder.

A Special Note About Front and Back Matter

Interestingly, your front and back matter files go in your Research Folder even though they may contain critical parts of your manuscript. Scrivener treats these files differently than others and there is a mechanism to compile front and back matter into your manuscript. Keeping the front and back matter sections separate from your manuscript ensures that your novel starts on page one, even when you have a dedication, acknowledgments, copyright information or a forward.

Files for the back matter work the same way as front matter folders. They are stored in the same location under the research portion of your Binder. You can have more than one option for back matter material. For example, you may want to include links to Amazon for your Kindle e-books and change those links to other sources when you go wide because retailers like Apple, Kobo and Barnes & Noble may not accept Amazon links.

If you use the novel template, Scrivener already has pre-made documents set up in the Binder to make the process easier.

Keeping your front and back matter separate makes it easier for you to update your manuscript as necessary.

I happen to use the same front matter regardless of whether I'm doing an e-book, a PDF, or Word document for my paperbacks. Other authors elect to have separate ones.

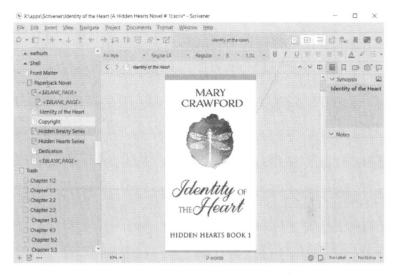

FIGURE 10: Front Matter in Research Folder Within Binder

If your books are on multiple marketing platforms, you can have one set of front and back matter which refers people to Amazon sites and another copy of the back matter which is free of any offending links. This will allow you to upload your book to different platforms such as Apple, Kobo, and Barnes & Noble.

If you are like me and you tend to use the same front and back matter, you can drag the folders from one project to another (if you don't already have it built into your template).

I also keep a copy of my e-book cover in the front matter folder to make it easy to locate when I'm ready to compile. If I want to, I can bookmark this file as a project bookmark. This is handy if you need to describe your cover models in detail for a certain scene.

The Trash Folder

The final mandatory file type is the Trash Folder. This folder is exactly what it sounds like. When you want to throw something away, you put it in the trash folder. It will stay in this folder until you empty the trash.

Do not empty the trash folder unless you are 100% certain you do not need the files or documents in it. Once the trash is emptied, you cannot retrieve your files.

If you want to delete specific files from your trash, select them in your binder and right-click. This will give you the option to delete them. Use this feature with caution because files deleted from the trash cannot be recovered.

Inspector

The Inspector is like the planner portion of the Trapper Keeper where you keep all your additional information to ensure your project goes smoothly. It is a bit of a catchall tool for external information applied to each individual document or file.

To access the Inspector, click on the blue I in the toolbar. Alternatively, you can use the keyboard shortcut (CTRL ⇧ I) to toggle the inspector on or off. You can also access the setting under View.

FIGURE 11: Inspector Icon in Scrivener 3 for Windows

If I am working on my laptop without my monitor, I will often switch off the binder and inspector since screen space can be limited.

Synopsis

The synopsis is where you can describe the chapter or section you're working on. This information can also appear in the outline. Each document or file in your binder will have its own synopsis.

If you change the name in the synopsis, it will also change in your binder and in the outline.

If you have more than one file selected in your binder, your synopsis will not show. Instead, you will be presented with the bookmark tab.

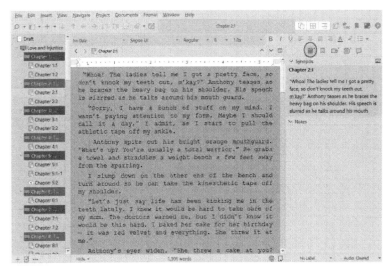

FIGURE 12: The Synopsis Within the Inspector Pane

In the example above, I have used the Auto Fill tool under Documents to automatically fill in the text under the chapter title. This tool populates the synopsis from the text you have written in your Scrivenings. Alternatively, you can place your main plot points in this area. Your synopsis will also appear on your index cards in the corkboard view. It is possible to add a picture to your synopsis. To add a picture to your synopsis, click on the picture in the upper right-hand corner then drag an image to the inspector. You can toggle back and forth between your picture or the written synopsis.

Placing a picture of your characters in your synopsis enables you to describe them more accurately.

The synopsis tab in the inspector also has a place for notes. I will often use this area to reinforce the story beats I want to hit in a particular chapter. After I've written my manuscript, I use this area to note any typos my beta readers found after editing.

Bookmarks

In a substantial upgrade to previous versions, Scrivener 3 for Windows has consolidated and replaced References, Project Notes and Favorites with Bookmarks.

Although this feature is easily overlooked, Bookmarks are very powerful.

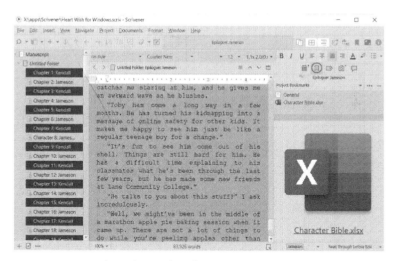

FIGURE 13: Bookmarks Within the Inspector Pane

In the example above, the bookmark section includes my character bible. Because I used the click and drag feature to place a link to my Excel spreadsheet into the bookmark area, I am able to click on the character bible and edit the original file.

This technique works phenomenally well if you are working with an external outlining or timeline program like Aeon Timeline or Scapple.

Unlike the Mac version, Scrivener 3 for Windows version does not give you a preview of the document in the notes area. However, if you click on the file in the bookmark, it will take you to your original document.

But that's not all the bookmarks can do. This new feature allows you to drag existing folders from your binder to the bookmarks. This is helpful if you are working with character sheets or need to have specific details from a chapter available with just a click.

To add a Bookmark quickly, click on the orange bookmark icon in the toolbar. Doing so will activate a window, and you can drag documents directly into it.

In addition to files from your Scrivener project, you can link to documents, websites, Excel files, databases, or calendars. Virtually anything you can drag into the bookmark area becomes a live, dynamic resource.

Bookmark setting can be reached by clicking the tab that looks like a ribbon in the Inspector pane, You can save a bookmark as either a document bookmark or a project bookmark by clicking on the down arrow next to the ellipsis. If you designate a bookmark as a project bookmark, it will be available for every file or document in your binder. This is very helpful for links to story bibles.

You can use more than one resource as a bookmark in any document or file. You just need to click and drag your material over to the bookmark area. To accomplish this, simply open

Windows Explorer and locate the file you want to use (if it's not already in your Scrivener project) and drag it to the top section of the bookmark. To bookmark a portion of your binder, just drag the folder over into the bookmark section you want to work with.

Be aware that if you rename an internal bookmark within your project, you are actually renaming the original file or folder.

Metadata

The metadata tab is often an underutilized function in the inspector. This tab looks a little like a price tag and it's between the bookmark and the snapshots.

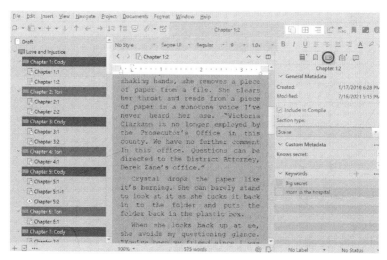

FIGURE 14: Metadata in Inspector

It allows you to see when a document or folder was created and the last time you modified it. I find this feature very helpful when I'm going back to edit a project. If you change something in a folder or document, the modified date will change.

Next, you can check a box to include this folder or document in your compile settings. So, if you write a document you don't want in your final output, just uncheck this box.

You can also assign section layouts. There will be a drop down list of available section layouts or you can add one of your own. I will discuss section layouts in detail in Chapter 5.

Custom metadata allows you to track specific data through each folder or document. For example, if I am writing a book which contains a secret that some characters know and others do not, I might use metadata to tell me which chapters discuss the big secret. You could also use this tool to track point of view, location or events on a timeline. You can elect to show your custom metadata in outline mode.

Setting up Custom Metadata is painless. Scrivener 3 for Windows makes it easy to add prepopulated lists, text, check boxes or dates.

You can add keywords to the next section. Keywords can appear in your outline or on the edge of your index cards. You can add keywords to track plots and subplots, time and location, the presence of certain characters in your document or folder. If you have a novel which changes tense, you might want to use keywords to indicate the switch. To add a new keyword, click on the +. If you want to delete a keyword you've already added, just use the subtract sign. You can click on the gear to show existing keywords or to add new ones.

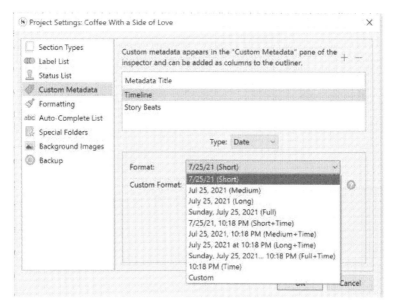

FIGURE 15: Setting up Custom Metadata Options

Snapshot

Snapshots is another one of the most overlooked features in Scrivener. I know I tend to make edits often, sometimes dramatically affecting my storyline. Using snapshots is an excellent way to keep track of your changes and compare them.

If you're not certain which direction you want to go with a character, and you want to try out an alternative storyline. No problem! Scrivener has you covered with snapshots.

Snapshots are a way for Scrivener to remember what you've just written and keep a copy—even when you write over the original manuscript with new information. If you don't like the changes you make, you can roll back to the version saved in your snapshot. You may have multiple snapshots of a single

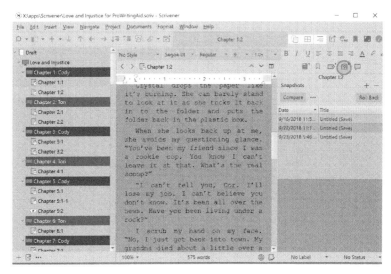

FIGURE 16: Snapshots Within the Inspector Pane

file within your binder. That's why it's a good idea to give each one a unique title.

You can place an icon in your toolbar which will allow you to save titled snapshots with just a click. Alternatively, Snapshots is the first menu item under Documents.

If I were to identify one feature in Scrivener I don't use nearly enough, it would be snapshots. Honestly, I forget the feature is available until after I've made changes and think to myself I should've taken a snapshot of that. So, if you are new to Scrivener 3 for Windows, it's a good idea to get in the habit of taking snapshots as you go along.

You can choose multiple files in your binder to include in your snapshots by pressing CTRL while you click on individual folders or documents in your binder.

Unfortunately, unlike the Mac version, you can't set your preferences to force Scrivener to take snapshots every time you open and close your files. So, if you want to use this method to compare versions, you'll need to remember to take snapshots before you make changes. I have taken the step to add a snapshot button to my toolbar to remind me to use this feature more often.

Comments & Footnotes

The last section in the inspector pane is the comments section. By highlighting a sentence or phrase and adding a comment, you can easily find it later to make edits or corrections. If you like to follow an outline, I recommend the comment feature to identify areas in which your characters decided to deviate from your carefully plotted ideas. This will help you identify areas which may lack cohesion in your final manuscript.

After you've addressed any issues you identified with comments, they can easily be deleted by pressing on the subtract sign.

You can change the color of your comments by right clicking on a comment you have made. For example, you might use one color for plot comments and another for grammar corrections which need to be made.

The comment icon looks like a speech bubble. Next to it, there are two small letters CF.

If you have your cursor in your Scrivenings window, you can click on these letters and add a footnote.

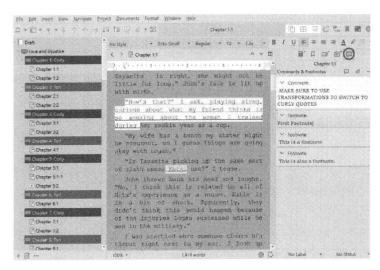

FIGURE 17: Comments and Footnotes in Scrivener

It is not hard to locate your footnotes in Scrivener 3 for Windows because they are clearly identified. You can change how your footnotes appear under Options (CTRL+) under Editing ▸ Formatting. Additionally, if you have used comments or footnotes, there will be a black dot next to the comment tab in the Inspector.

Although the focus of this book skews toward writing novels, I'm aware Scrivener can be used for more academic pursuits. That's okay. Scrivener has several templates for different types of work including academic projects and they provide more direct guidance on using footnotes than the novel templates.

It is easy to identify which sections have footnotes in the inspector. There will be a dot beside the comment tab if your folder or document contains footnotes or comments.

Removing a comment or footnote is as easy as clicking the subtract sign in the inspector.

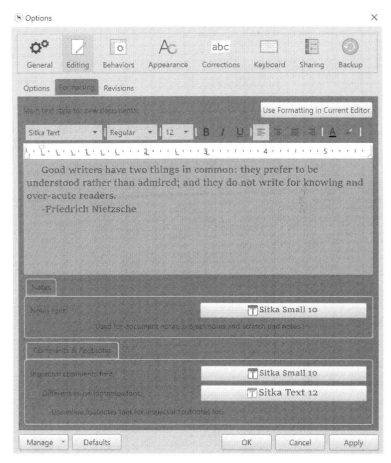

FIGURE 18: Changing Font and Size of Footnotes

Scrivener also allows you to export your comments to an external file. To use this feature, click on File ▸ Export ▸ Comments & Annotations. This is helpful if you are working with an external reference manager program. Speaking of working with an external reference manager, you can set one up under Options (CTRL+) ▸ General ▸ Citations.

Unfortunately, unlike the Mac version, it is not currently possible to export footnotes with Scrivener 3 for Windows. I expect that Literature and Latte may fix this in future updates.

Now that I have discussed the various portions of the inspector function, I will turn to Group Mode.

Group Mode

The group mode refers to the way you view your manuscript in Scrivener. There are three views included in the group mode. The first is the Document Mode which is represented by a piece of paper. If you have more than one folder or file selected in your binder, Scrivener 3 for Windows displays the result as Scrivenings. Therefore, you will often hear the Document Mode referred to as Scrivenings.

The second view is the Corkboard Mode. If you squint, you can envision its icon as representing index cards on a corkboard. The third view is the Outlining Mode. It is represented by blue lines of different shades. Abstractly, it looks like an outline. This group mode appears by default on your toolbar. The mode you have selected will be highlighted. In this case, I am in the Document Mode. You can also use keyboard shortcuts to get to each view in group mode. The Scrivenings Mode can be accessed by pushing CTRL 1. If you wish to be in Corkboard Mode, press CTRL 2. To switch to outline view, use CTRL 3.

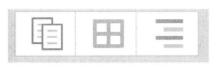

FIGURE 19: Group Mode in Scrivener 3

If you have your binder and your inspector open, the middle pane is referred to as the editor window. This window has a different appearance depending upon which group mode you are operating in. You can have changes made in your corkboard appear in your binder. Alternatively, if you just want to experiment with the corkboard without impacting your binder, you do not have to commit the changes to the binder. I will discuss the functions included in the corkboard mode in Chapter 10.

Scrivenings

I'll admit, when I first was watching tutorials about Scrivener, I was confused about the term Scrivenings. It's actually a rather exotic term used to describe the portion of Scrivener which looks like a word processor. This is also referred to as Document Mode. Unfortunately, these terms are used interchangeably in different parts of Scrivener 3 for Windows documentation and file menus.

You can write directly in the Document Mode and do all the typical things you would usually do in a word processing program. You can format your words as bold, italic or underline. You can change the justification, color, and line spacing.

The line spacing function looks a little different from other word processing programs. The setting is located right after the font size on the formatting bar. It is relatively straightforward to use.

In the Scrivenings window, if you have a document with several sub documents, they will be displayed with section dividers on the screen. Most commonly, this is displayed as a dashed line. However, you can easily change the default setting. The appearance of this divider can be changed under Options (CTRL+). The setting is found under the General tab.

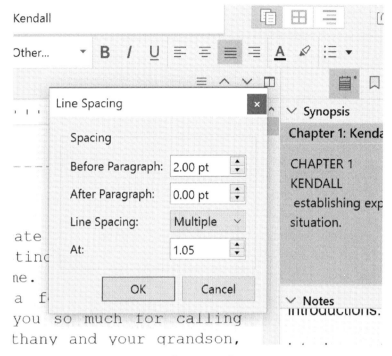

FIGURE 20: Line spacing in Scrivener 3

The Document Mode is one of many places you can assign Scrivener's new style feature. Styles are the way you tell Scrivener how you want your words to appear. This includes things like font choice, spacing, special formatting like small caps and justification. I will be discussing them in greater detail in Chapter 5.

You can also change the font or font size in the Scrivenings page without applying a style.

If you choose N/A when you are compiling, Scrivener will use your default settings to determine the appearance of each folder or document.

Speaking of formatting, indenting using tabs or manual spacing is problematic when you produce e-books. It is preferable to use the ruler to set your margins and indents. Next, we'll talk about rulers, which make this task much easier.

Using the Ruler

Using tabs and manual spacing can disrupt your formatting in e-books. Therefore, it's best not to use them.

Scrivener's solution to this is the ruler.

The ruler allows you to set indents and margins without using tabs.

To make the ruler appear, either place an icon for it on your toolbar or press CTRL ⇧ R. (Don't forget the shift key in this keyboard shortcut or you will end up right justifying your text). You can also find this on the menu under View ▸ Text Editing ▸ Ruler.

Unlike some word processors, the ruler in Scrivener 3 for Windows starts at zero. This setting is calibrated to where your text starts, not to the edge of the paper. You will need to adjust your margins accordingly.

FIGURE 21: Ruler with Margins and Indent Shown

To set an indent, drag the inverted triangle at the top of the ruler to the depth you would like your paragraphs to be indented. The same concept applies to setting your margins. Just drag the triangles from either end to the measurements you prefer.

Using the ruler to set your margins and indents makes it easier to format your book in the end.

Outline Mode

One of Scrivener's three group modes is the Outlining Mode. As with other areas of Scrivener, if you change the title of one of the folders or documents in your outline, it will appear on the cards in the corkboard view and in your binder. For the outline feature to work properly, you need to select a folder in your binder which has some documents.

To make the outline mode appear, click on the icon in your toolbar with the blue lines or press CTRL 3. You can expand or collapse your outline by using ALT [and ALT], or by clicking the expand and collapse icons in your toolbar if you have cus-tomized it to include them.

As you can see in figure 22, I have the outline displayed with the synopsis information automatically generated from my text. You can toggle the synopsis on and off by clicking on the button at the bottom of the screen on the right-hand side. Additionally, you can choose which information to display in your outline mode by clicking on the button which looks like a ▸ on the top

FIGURE 22: Outline Pane with Synopsis Showing

right-hand side of the window. This symbol appears right next to the Inspector if you are displaying the Inspector window. Choose which options you want to display in the outline pane. In the figure above, I have added columns for targets, word counts and date modified. Additionally, you can reach this menu by choosing View ‣ Outliner Options.

One of the new features introduced in Scrivener 3 allows you to change your styles from the outline pane. Sometimes, it's easier to see which format to use when you can get an overview of your whole document. Changing the styles in the outline pane also changes them in the binder and the corkboard pane. This is also true if you add more files or change the synopsis information while in the outline pane.

You can work with your manuscript in the outline pane, just like you would if you were writing an outline on paper. To add a new folder, just click on the folder with the + in the lower left-hand corner located on the footer tool bar.

You can press CTRL N for a new document or CTRL⇧N for a new folder. This shortcut works in the binder, corkboard pane or outline pane.

You can move folders within your outline with either the arrow buttons in your tool bar or by pressing CTRL↑, CTRL ↓, CTRL→ or CTRL←. However, there is a limit to the number of levels you can move using the keyboard shortcuts. If you've reached this limit, the folders or documents will not move.

I will discuss more advanced features of the Outline Mode in Chapter 11.

The Corkboard Mode is another view within group mode which lets you see in different levels. Some authors prefer to work with index cards and sticky notes. The corkboard has many helpful features to move your planning to the digital world.

Corkboard

If you are a fan of working with index cards or sticky notes to organize (or reorganize) your manuscript, the Corkboard pane might be for you. This feature in Scrivener is exactly what it sounds like. It is a mode that allows you to view your manuscript as electronic index cards. If you wish, you can even change the background of your index cards, so they resemble traditional cards.

Although the outline mode and corkboard mode present your manuscript in different formats, many of the keyboard shortcuts that are applicable to the outline pane are the same in the corkboard pane.

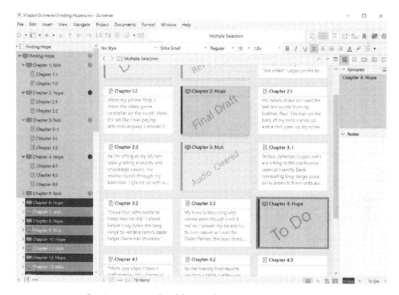

FIGURE 23: Scrivener in Corkboard View

To enter the Corkboard view, click on the orange box with four white squares in the group mode on the toolbar (or press CTRL 2). It is important to remember that you need to be in a folder with sub-folders for this feature to work properly. I usually work from the folder which contains all my other folders when I work in Corkboard Mode so I can see the whole document. The colors I use in my labels determine the colors of the index cards. You can turn off this feature. The stamps are determined by the status I assigned each section on the footer bar. You can toggle the stamp feature on and off with F10. You can also choose the opacity of the stamp under Options (CTRL+).

The stack with multiple cards is used to indicate it is a folder or document with sub-folders or sub documents. If the subfolders are not showing, click on the folder on the index card. Doing this will open up the sub-folders or sub documents.

 To see all your index cards at once, highlight the folders and subfolders in your binder before you click on the Corkboard view and your subfolders will appear on your corkboard.

In Scrivener 3, there is a new view for the Corkboard pane. You can elect to show your cards in a new format called Arrange by Label. There is an option to switch between vertical and horizontal. This feature can be handy when tracking time, location or points of view. In the example below, my story has several points of view. So, I can see where each index card appears in relation to other points of view. You can toggle back and forth between the traditional view and Arrange by Label without affecting your manuscript.

In Arrange By Label view, changing the label of your folder or document is as simple as dragging it to another label color on the Corkboard.

The corkboard also has two modes for manipulating index cards (other than arrange by label). One is a traditional arrangement of your index cards. In this mode, if you make changes to the order of your index cards, the order of files in your binder and outline also change.

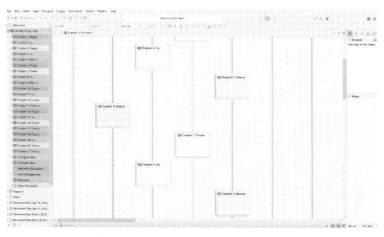

FIGURE 24: Corkboard Arrange by Label View

If you don't want your changes to automatically apply, you can elect to go into Free-Form view. If you are in this view, the changes you make in the corkboard don't appear in your binder or outline until you click the commit button. This feature is incredibly helpful when you are moving around scenes and chapters to see where they fit best. You can experiment without affecting your binder or outline. When your index cards are to your liking, you can click on the commit button. Your Binder and Outline will be rearranged accordingly.

After you've worked with your manuscript in one of the group modes, you probably want to compile your results. Although it seems like a scary term, compile is just the name Literature and Latte has given to the process of collecting all of your individual documents and creating a cohesive document for use in Microsoft Word, PDF, or e-book (among many other formats). I'll give an overview of the compile function next.

Compile

Of all the features in Scrivener 3, the most changed from the prior version is the compiler (CTRL ⇧ E). For those of you who are new to Scrivener, compile is the way you tell Scrivener to put together the parts of your manuscript. This is one of the hardest concepts for many users of Scrivener to grasp.

 The compile feature allows you to change the appearance of your output without having to physically change your manuscript.

 The compile feature is uniquely powerful because you can output your manuscript as several file types such as .PDF, .EPUB, .MOBI, or .DOCX without having to use an external program.

Learning to compile will save you copious amounts of time. I will discuss compile in depth in Chapter 11, but I will give a brief description and overview here.

I understand the compile feature looks hopelessly complicated. When I first used it, I'd never seen anything like it, and I struggled to understand the concept. Hopefully, I can simplify it for you so it is not so intimidating. To open the compile feature, click on your toolbar or press CTRL ⇧ E. Alternatively, you can use the menu and choose File ▸ Compile.

As you can see in the figures below, your compile pane can look different depending on the type of file you are creating, the format you choose and which section layouts you include. For example, the top window contains the settings I use when I write nonfiction. The next figure shows my custom format I've developed for my fiction novels. In this case, it is showing the options for my Hidden Beauty Series.

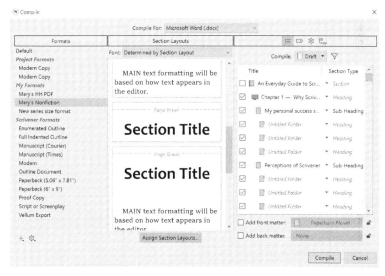

FIGURE 25: Compile Window in Scrivener 3

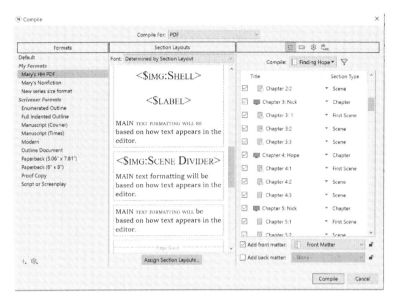

FIGURE 26: Custom Format in the Compile Window in Scrivener 3

On the surface, the compiler looks incredibly different from earlier versions. However, many parts of it function the same way as it used to. There are four main parts to the compiler menu. At the very top, you choose which type of output you would like to create.

At the top of the menu, choose the output of your manuscript. I most commonly use Microsoft .DOCX or .EPUB. However, there are more than a dozen output options to choose from.

The options in the left-hand side of the window under format change depending on which output method you choose. The formats provided by Scrivener have pre-populated options in them based on their function. You can always change a Scrivener format to customize it to your needs. Formats can be saved to each individual project or globally.

If you want to share your
Scrivener file with someone
else and you want them to be
able to see exactly how you
formatted it, you need to save
your format as a Project Format
instead of under My Formats.

On the right-hand side of the Compiler Window is the list
of folders or documents in your project. You simply check the
ones you want to have included in your output.

If you want to select all the files
in the Compile Pane press ALT
while you click in the checkbox.

All of your documents in this window will have a Section
Type attached. If the wrong Section Type appears, click on the
down arrow and choose another Section Layout from the menu.
If for some reason your manuscript is not compiling correctly,
this is one place to look for mistakes.

In the above figure, I am compiling an .EPUB file so I don't
need any blank pages like I do when I am formatting a paperback. Therefore, I unchecked those boxes.

There are other options in this pane which I will discuss
later in Chapter 11.

In Scrivener 3, the middle pane is new. In this window, you
assign section formats to your project format.

The compile function in Scrivener 3 is phenomenally flexible.
You can customize your formats to include several types of fonts,

graphics, font effects, line spacing, or colors. This is accomplished through the application of different Section Types. This process is slightly different from earlier versions of Scrivener and it takes a bit of time to set up. However, the good news is once you set up the format and assign Section Types, you can use them over and over again.

When you choose a different type of output, the available format options change. For example, you will have different formats available if you choose .EPUB for an e-book or a Microsoft document or .PDF for paperback.

Export your formats and save them in a safe place like a USB drive in case your favorite format gets corrupted.

I've had this happen before. Fortunately, I had exported my formats and was able to delete the corrupt one and use the working one.

Remember when I was discussing the Scrivenings window? I briefly discussed applying Section Layouts to each folder or document. The compiler is where it all comes together.

In the left-hand side of the window are the formats. This is how you tell Scrivener what you want your manuscript to look like. If you right-click on the Format, you can edit it.

I recommend that you duplicate the format before you edit it. If you choose Duplicate Format, you will be given the opportunity to save it.

You can either save it as a Project Format, which attaches it only to the particular project you are working on, or you can save it to my formats which makes it globally available.

Clicking on Edit Format or Duplicate and Edit brings you to a window that you might recognize from Scrivener 2. Your Section Layouts are listed in this window. You can add or subtract different types of Section Layouts here. You need to set your preferences for each type of Section Layout you plan to use. In this particular project, I am only using five of the six different section layouts available in this format. They are indicated in bold.

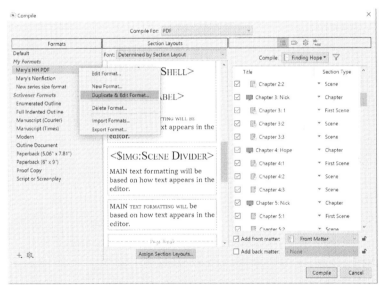

FIGURE 27: Editing Formats in Compile Window

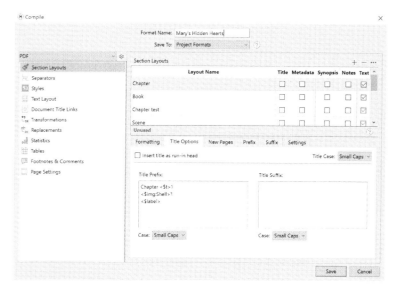

FIGURE 28: Editing Format Options in Scrivener 3

You can make changes to several Section Layouts in this window. However, make sure to click save when you're done.

If you create a new Section Type while you are in compile, in order for the system to work properly, you need to add it to the Section Layout menu. To do this, simply right click on one of your folders and go down to Edit. When you click Edit, a window listing all of your Section Types will appear. Just click the plus sign and add the title of your section. Although, the names do not need to be identical; it helps improve clarity if you name them something similar.

From this menu, you can also add new labels or status types as well as things you want to track with custom metadata.

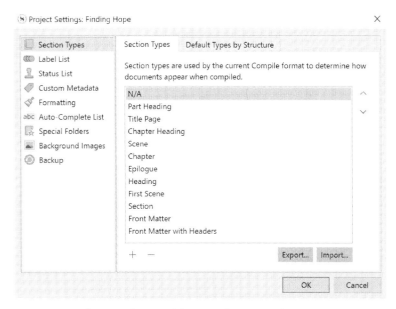

FIGURE 29: Section Layout Menu in Scrivener 3

Scrivener 3 has a new feature which was not present in Scrivener 2. This is the middle pane where you assign layouts to your Format. Think of this as different parts of Scrivener shaking hands. You've already determined which Section Layout you want for each document or folder in your Binder, now assigning section formats will tell Scrivener which Section Layout goes with each specific option in your format.

If you haven't assigned your section layouts to a specific format, you will see a yellow warning label advising you to assign your layouts.

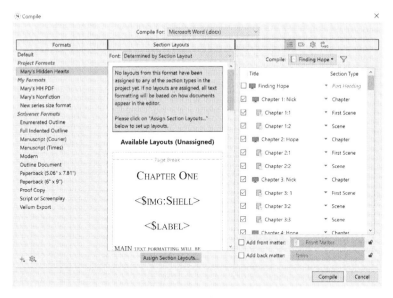

FIGURE 30: Assign Section Layout Warning

Once you click on Assign Section Layouts, Scrivener 3 will bring up a window like in Figure 31.

If you right-click on the options in the left-hand pane, it brings up a drop-down menu which makes it easy to choose which Section Layout you want to apply. Alternatively, you can just click on the style you want for each Section Type.

In Chapter 11, I will have a thorough discussion of all the features in Compile. This section is meant to be an overview to highlight the changes between older versions of Scrivener and the update to Scrivener 3.

One of the most popular features in Scrivener is its ability to block out all distractions while you write. In the next section, I will discuss the Compose Window.

FIGURE 31: Assigning Layouts Within Scrivener 3

Compose

Distraction is the bane of authors everywhere. Scrivener has a cure for that. It's called the Compose Mode. You can click on the composition button in the toolbar or use F11. This is a toggle command, but you can also use the escape key to get back to your normal view in Scrivener. You can also find this option under the view menu.

This mode has a very minimal display. However, if you need to do things like change the style of your document or assign a section layout, those options are available to you. Additionally, you can change the paper size and where it is presented on your screen. For me, this particular option is very helpful because I have cerebral palsy and I write from bed. My monitor isn't lined up perfectly within my line of sight. In composition mode, I can place the paper on the right-hand side of the monitor which makes it easier for me to see.

 My other favorite feature in composition mode is typewriter scrolling. It means no matter how much you type, your cursor will stay in the center of your paper. This feature is now available in the main editor as well (except in page view). No more scrolling!

I find that I am more productive when I use this mode. Primarily, this is because I'm not reminded of the dozen other things I need to do on my computer while I am writing. On my wish list for the makers of Scrivener, Literature and Latte, is a timer in this mode for those of us who like to sprint. When I write in the compose mode, I use the timer on my phone instead of the one on the computer.

If you would like to use your own background image, you can easily add one. To do this, click on Project Settings under the Project menu. I use covers of my books so that if I need to describe a facial feature or something it's right there in front of me.

A menu bar automatically comes into view if you move your mouse along the bottom of the screen. The Go To menu will allow you to go anywhere in your Binder and the Inspector button will pull up your Inspector window if you need to consult your notes or other details about your folder or document. There is a word count visible on the toolbar. You can display this toolbar or automatically hide it. The choice is yours. This setting is also found in Options (CTRL+).

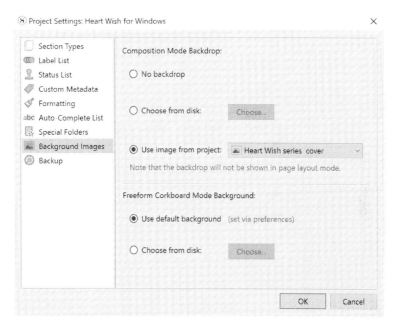

FIGURE 32: Adding a Background to Your Composition Mode in Scrivener 3 for Windows

Copyholders

If you want to consult a document or a photograph briefly, you can open it as a copyholder. Copyholder allows you to have up to four documents open for reference. In essence, they serve as clipboards within your editing pane. You can edit copyholder documents directly. Unlike other editing panes, your changes won't effect other areas of your project.

To open a copyholder within your editing pane, go to Navigate ▸ Open ▸ in Copyholder on the menu. Alternatively, you can right-click on an item in your binder and choose Open ▸ in Copyholder. After your copyholder is open, you can right-click on the title bar and select the location where you want the copyholder window to appear.

Scriptwriting Mode

I don't work in Scriptwriting Mode because I write fiction. I've never written a script. However, for those of you who do scriptwriting in Scrivener, it can be a valuable tool.

When you first open a project in Scrivener, in addition to fiction, nonfiction and academic options, there are several templates available for scriptwriting. These templates come pre-populated with options to make screenwriting easier. To enter Scriptwriting Mode, press CTRL 8 or Scriptwriting under the Format menu. When you do this, the Footer Status Bar changes to include new options. CTRL 4 functions like a toggle switch. When you press CTRL 4 again, you will return to the standard writing mode.

When you apply these options to your text, it formats it in the proper screenwriting format.

FIGURE 33: Sample of Screenwriting Mode

The Footer Status Bar will offer matting different parts of your script.

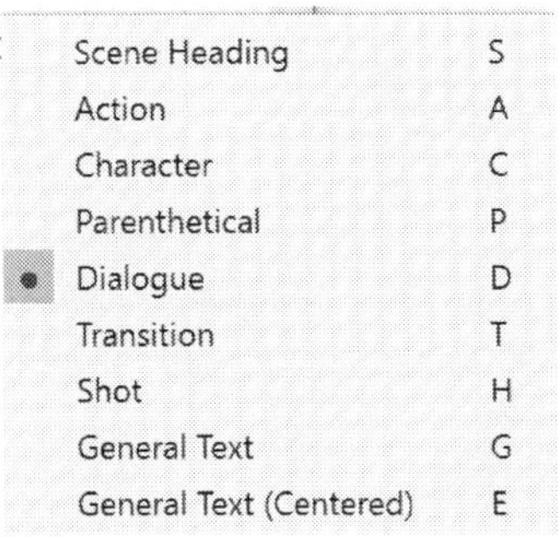

Scene Heading	S
Action	A
Character	C
Parenthetical	P
● Dialogue	D
Transition	T
Shot	H
General Text	G
General Text (Centered)	E

Allowing Scrivener to automatically apply the proper formatting for each part of your script will speed up the process. If you hit enter at the end of the line, Scrivener will take you to the next element. Or, if you tab at the beginning of the line, it will toggle between different elements.

FIGURE 34: Default Options in Scriptwriting Mode

When you're finished, the default output method and compile for scriptwriting mode is Front Page. However, you can output to other file types such as PDFs or Word documents.

Literature and Latte offers some helpful videos with examples and tips on using scriptwriting mode.

Now that we have explored many of the moving parts which make Scrivener a powerful piece of software, we're going to talk about how to customize it to work with your preferences. After all, these are your tools and they should suit your style of writing.

CHAPTER 3

Making Scrivener Your Own

Scrivener is one of the most customizable programs I've ever used. There isn't much you can't change to accommodate your tastes. The philosophy behind Scrivener is that everyone has a different writing process. So, Scrivener 3 for Windows is eminently flexible. For example, I am a fan of customizing my toolbar and having everything at my disposal, while other writers much prefer using keyboard shortcuts. Still others prefer to navigate through menus. Scrivener allows you to do all of those things. You can customize the appearance of virtually everything in Scrivener.

Before Scrivener introduced their dark mode, I used to create different backgrounds for each project I was working on. I have worked on as many as four projects at once. It is nice to be able to tell them apart by just looking at the appearance of the project in front of me. To a certain extent, I still do this by changing the label colors of each character. (I typically write in first-person, alternating points of view, when I write fiction.) Changing the label colors allows me to know at a glance which project is open.

The default settings are easily changed and apply to all of your projects.

You can also set personal targets and deadlines and track your progress in Scrivener 3. There are new ways to visualize your progress without having to open other tools or windows.

You may have noticed that Scrivener 3 for Windows has keyboard shortcuts for many things. In the section about keyboard shortcuts, I will provide a list of keyboard shortcuts to serve as a quick reference guide.

Toolbars are one of the most helpful features in Scrivener 3. We will discuss those next.

Customizing the Toolbar

A lot of features in Scrivener don't appear in other word processing programs. Therefore, the toolbar becomes an invaluable resource. You can display only icons or have the names of the tools appear below the icon. If you hover your mouse over each button, there is usually a helpful tooltip attached to help you navigate Scrivener 3 for Windows more efficiently.

To customize your toolbar, click on the View menu and then on Customize Toolbars.

If you are new to Scrivener, you may not know which options you will use most often on your toolbar. That's okay. You can add or subtract items from your toolbar when you get a better feel for which tools you use most often.

This window is made up of three parts. On the upper right side, you have the option to modify your main toolbar or the format toolbar. On the left side, are the options available for each toolbar. The lower right side lists the contents of your current toolbar.

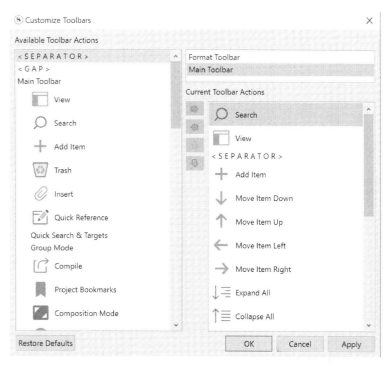

FIGURE 35: Options Under Customize Toolbar

To add a tool to your toolbar, click the right facing blue arrow. If you want, you can use the up and down arrows to move items on your toolbar. You can also adjust the spacing options choosing SEPARATOR or GAP, if you wish. Conversely, if you want to remove a tool from your toolbar, just click on the tool in your current toolbar list and click on the left facing blue arrow. Never fear, if you want to put it back, it will be available from the icon menu.

There are some toolbar options I find indispensable. The move buttons which help you determine which level your document or folder is located in the Binder are useful. I also add the expand and collapse tools because I use them frequently. Another helpful tool is the layout button. It allows you to instantly switch the layout of your editing windows to include different things, such as the outline or the corkboard. Additionally, it leads to another menu which allows you to analyze the frequency of word usage.

On the formatting bar, I find it helpful to add an option for undo and redo.

Scrivener has several types of redundancies built in. Often, there are three or four ways to accomplish nearly every task or feature Scrivener offers. The toolbar is only one mechanism for accessing these features. They are accessible via the menu or through keyboard shortcuts.

The toolbar is not the only area of Scrivener you can customize. You can also alter the appearance of the Scrivener interface to suit your needs.

Color your World ... or Not

I'll admit, I'm a very visual person. I love having the ability to customize my work environment to suit my project or even my mood. Fortunately, Scrivener 3 makes this process much easier. They have pre-existing themes available in both light and dark mode. Although the pictures I've taken for this book are made using the light mode, when I don't have to document the steps I take and insert them into a book, I write in dark mode.

I am a chronic migraine sufferer. I started getting migraines in 2002. The ability to change the colors of the program I'm working in has radically increased my ability to work in front of the computer without pain. Before Scrivener introduced dark modes, I used to create them on my own by changing each element of Scrivener to a custom color. Thanks to the built-in settings in dark mode, I no longer have to do this.

How you choose your project in Scrivener 3 for Windows to appear on your screen doesn't have to have any bearing on the output of your manuscript. Feel free to write using colors you love. Later, I'll show you how to ensure the compile feature doesn't use any odd colors you write with.

I find it easier to customize my Scrivener interface if I start with a theme which is closest to how I want my projects to appear and then adapt it.

Themes are located under Window on the menu. Scrivener 3 for Windows has included both light and dark themes. Although I have used light themes in the illustrations of this book, I prefer to write using dark themes.

Make sure you have saved your work before trying to apply a new theme because it is likely you'll need to restart Scrivener in order to apply it.

If the options available don't suit your fancy, check out the bulletin boards on Literature and Latte. They have several themes uploaded by users. You may have to unzip the file before you can import your new theme and, as always, when you download something from an unknown source, make sure you run a virus check. It's very easy to import a theme. When you do, it will appear on the menu of themes.

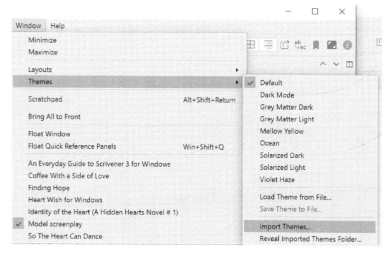

FIGURE 36: Importing Themes in Scrivener 3 for Windows

If you want to develop your own theme, start with one that's closest to how you want your final theme to appear. Then go to Options (CTRL+). Click on the Appearance tab and a menu of choices will appear. Choose Colors and another menu will appear. Make sure you click on the triangles beside each word to expose more options.

To change color, simply click on the color box above the Use Default Color button. That will bring up a panel of colors you can choose from. I have noticed occasionally that the color won't change when I click on it. If this happens to you, simply drag the color you want to choose into the existing color box. Then, it should change.

FIGURE 37: Changing Colors Under Options in Scrivener 3 for Windows

Once you have changed all the options you wish, click on the Manage button and save your theme. Additionally, you can save the changes to a particular file if you don't want what you created to be applied globally.

As with all other types of customization and personal settings, I recommend that you export these items and save them on a thumb drive or an external backup drive. If something catastrophic happens to your computer or the Scrivener program, having these settings saved separately will help you restore your writing environment. Optimally, you should save both your options and your theme. To access this menu, click on Manage.

FIGURE 38: Saving Customized Preferences and Themes in Scrivener 3 for Windows

Creating themes with your preferences for color and font is only one method for customizing your experience on Scrivener 3. Another key area involves setting the default behavior and settings for Document Mode (sometimes referred to as Scrivenings).

Changing and Setting Defaults

Scrivener's behavior and appearance depends a lot on its default settings for the editor. Of course, in several places Scrivener gives you the opportunity to override your default settings with an alternative font. Still, it's helpful to set up your default editor in the style you prefer. If you choose N/A as your style layout in compile, whatever is in your default editor will appear. Basically, this is an as-is setting.

To change the default settings, choose File ▸ Options to access the menu. From there, you will see the Edit tab. The first option is the Options menu. This allows you to set a few key settings including your default zoom, use of overwrite, and how footnotes are handled.

When you change the default settings, it does not affect projects you've already finished. Changes only apply to new projects.

My eyesight has never been spectacular. So, I appreciate the ability to set my default zoom at 250%. Additionally, I like to have my typewriter scroll appear in the middle of the window.

The next menu tab is Formatting. This allows you to determine how new documents will appear in Scrivener.

You can set these preferences manually by making changes in the edit window in the Options (CTRL+) menu. You can do things like set margins, default fonts, colors and spacing—like you would in any word processing program. If you are a fan of Microsoft Word, the default setting is similar to the normal template in Word.

You can also set the format of your footnotes in this section.

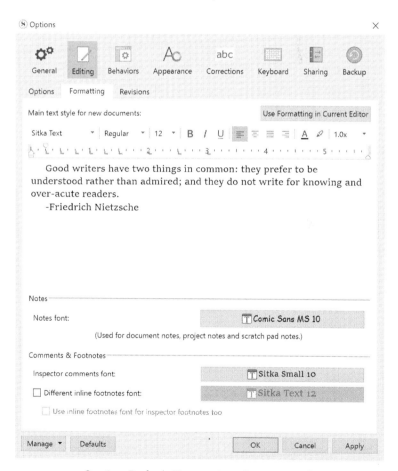

FIGURE 39: Setting Default Formatting Options under Preferences in Scrivener 3

Although you can set up settings for things like margins, line spacing, fonts and indents manually, if you have another documents in Scrivener where the settings are to your liking, you can open that document and set your preferences while in that document. Choose Edit, and then Formatting. Once you are on that window, choose Use Formatting in Current Editor. This button will make the formatting in your document apply to all new documents.

If you have made substantial changes in this window, it is a good idea to save your preferences in a location separate from your computer's hard drive. To do this, click on the Manage button and choose Save Options.

The last tab under editing menu is revisions. This allows you to apply custom colors to revision options. It is a common misconception that Scrivener has no way to track your changes when you are revising a document. You can show which text you add or subtract by choosing a revision color.

Revision Mode is located under the Format menu. When you go into Revision Mode, any changes you make will be in the revision color you choose. You can change these colors to suit your needs by clicking on File ▸ Options ▸ Editing ▸ Revisions. To change colors, just click on each color and a color selection tool will be displayed.

Unlike track changes in Microsoft Word, Scrivener doesn't make changes for you. In the revision mode, it just keeps track of the changes you have made

After you have your writing environment customized to your taste, and you have set up the default settings for the editor, it is helpful to have a way to measure your progress on your manuscript. Scrivener 3 for Windows allows for different types of targets. I will discuss setting up targets to measure your progress in the next section.

Targets, Deadlines and Progress

As I have mentioned before, I am a sprinter. I like to keep track of how many words I write in a session. Fortunately, Scrivener makes this task easy.

 The new quick search tool in Scrivener 3 makes it possible to see a visual representation of your progress toward your targets at a single glance.

It is great positive reinforcement to see the line indicating progress continue to grow and change colors throughout the process.

As you can see in the figure below, it is still early in my writing day and I have written only fifty words this morning. I am a little under three quarters finished with the word target I project for this book. The top line represents my overall progress. The bottom line represents how much progress toward my goals I've made today. As you get closer to meeting your targets, the color will change. To meet my deadline, I need to write 250 words today. Of course, I'm crazy competitive with myself and I often try to beat the minimum number.

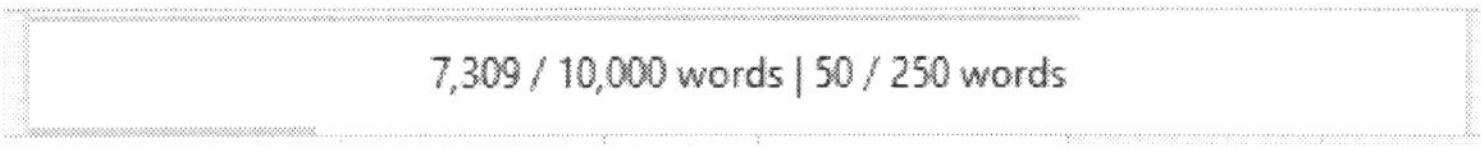

7,309 / 10,000 words | 50 / 250 words

FIGURE 40: Progress Indicators in Quick Search Box in Scrivener 3 for Windows

To make this feature work properly, you need to set up the targets in your project. I have the target icon in my toolbar, but you can also get there by pressing CTRL, or clicking on Project and then Show Project Targets.

By clicking on the options button, you can choose which documents to include in your count and set your deadline. If you click on session targets, you can choose the time at which you want the counts to reset and whether you will allow negative counts. Negative counts occur when you go back and edit your work and delete words. Unless I am shooting for a very specific word count, I often turn this feature off once I hit the editing stage. Sometimes, I just don't want to know how many of my words I've deleted.

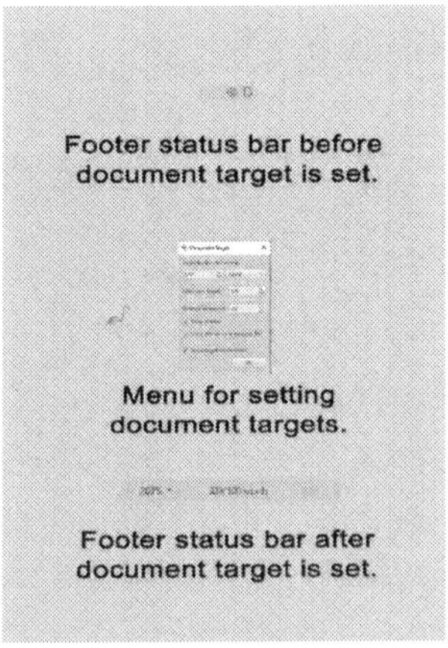

Footer status bar before document target is set.

Menu for setting document targets.

Footer status bar after document target is set.

FIGURE 41: Setting Document Targets in Scrivener 3

You can also set targets for each individual document, folder, sub-document or sub-folder. You can have your progress displayed in Outline Mode and down at the bottom of your screen in the footer status bar.

To set a target for an individual document or folder, click on the target and a menu will appear which allows you to set your target as well as a minimum target and a maximum overrun.

I don't know if this will show up in the print or Kindle version, but if you'll notice on the aqua line there is a smaller vertical line. This line indicates you have set a minimum target for this folder or document.

 If you set a target before you duplicate your folder or document, the target will be duplicated as well.

If you have a project you use as a template, those targets will be saved from project to project.

For some reason, sometimes it doesn't work to click on the target while in Document Mode. If this happens to you, you can also set document targets in the Outline Mode.

If you are interested in sprints (a method of timed writing which greatly increases your productivity), I have put some links to sprinting resources in the resource guide at the end of this book.

Scrivener 3 has another tool, writing history, to track your progress. It is located under Project (CTRL ,). It allows you to track your progress on your manuscript day by day.

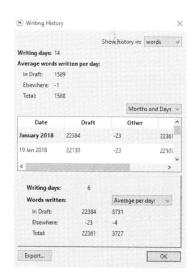

FIGURE 42: Writing History in Scrivener 3 for Windows

Project targets are a great way to motivate yourself and keep track of your progress. Scrivener has many ways to help make your work more efficient. Keyboard shortcuts are one of those tools. We'll be discussing those next.

Keyboard Shortcuts

The great thing about Scrivener is it doesn't pin you down to one way to accomplish something. For example, if you want to add a new folder to your Binder, there are about five ways to accomplish this. You can click on the big green + in the toolbar, or, you can click on the + in the footer status bar, or you can add it under Project in the menu, or you can right-click on an existing folder in your Binder and click on add. The keyboard shortcut CTRL ⇧ N will also create a new folder.

This is only one example. The same holds true for many of the key functions in Scrivener. Fortunately, many of the keyboard shortcuts are listed in the menu.

For your convenience, I have provided an alphabetical chart of several of the keyboard shortcuts available in Scrivener 3 for Windows.

Be aware that if another program which is simultaneously running with Scrivener is using the same keyboard shortcuts for one of their functions, you may have difficulty using the keyboard shortcut assigned to Scrivener. For example, the keyboard shortcut to start a new project starts an Xbox toolbar when I try to use it. If I cared enough about using keyboard shortcuts, I could change it in either application. Most of the time, I work through my toolbars. Therefore, I don't bother.

CTRL+X, CTRL+Y simply means hold down the CTRL key then typing XY.

You can add or change any existing shortcut keys in Scrivener via File ▸ Options ▸ Keyboard.

Meta or WK is the Windows key normally to the right of the space bar.

KEY CHART

- ALT = Alt Key
- WK or Meta = Windows Key
- CTRL = Control Key
- ⌫ = Delete Key
- ↓ = Down Arrow Key
- ⏎ = Return Key
- ← = Left Arrow Key
- → = Right Arrow Key
- ⇧ = Shift Key
- ⇥ = Tab Key
- ↑ = Up Arrow Key

DOCUMENT

- Duplicate Item with Subdocuments: CTRL+D
- Duplicate Item without Subdocuments: CTRL+⇧+D
- Group Selection: CTRL+G, CTRL+U

- Merge Documents: CTRL+G, CTRL+M
- Move Item Down: CTRL+Alt+Down
- Move Item Down: CTRL+Down
- Move Item Left: CTRL+Alt+Left
- Move Item Left: CTRL+Left
- Move Item Right: CTRL+Alt+Right
- Move Item Right: CTRL+Right
- Move Item Up: CTRL+Alt+Up
- Move Item Up: CTRL+Up
- Move to Trash: ⇧+Del
- Open in Editor: CTRL+⇧+Return
- Open in External Editor: CTRL+F5
- Open in Other Editor: CTRL+Alt+Return
- Set Selection as Title: F2
- Split at Selection: CTRL+K
- Split with Selection as Title: CTRL+⇧+K
- Take Snapshot with Title: CTRL+⇧+5
- Take Snapshot: CTRL+5
- UnGroup Selection: CTRL+⇧+U

EDIT

- Add Current to Completions: CTRL+G, CTRL+A
- Apply Last Highlight Color: CTRL+⇧+H
- Apply Last Text Color: CTRL+G, CTRL+H
- Complete Current Title: Alt++
- Complete Current Word: Alt+=
- Copy: CTRL+C
- Find by Format Dialog: CTRL+F3
- Find Dialog: CTRL+F
- Find Next by Format: CTRL+⇧+F3
- Find Previous by Format: CTRL+Alt+F3
- Ignore Spelling: CTRL+G, CTRL+I
- Insert Current Date and Time: CTRL+F6

- Insert Image: CTRL+J
- Insert Line Break: CTRL+G, CTRL+Y
- Insert Non-Breaking Space: CTRL+⇧+Space
- Insert Page Break: CTRL+G, CTRL+Z Cut: CTRL+X
- Jump to Selection: CTRL+G, CTRL+W
- Learn Spelling: CTRL+G,
- Paste and Match Style: CTRL+⇧+V
- Paste: CTRL+V
- Quick Search: CTRL+⇧+G
- Redo: CTRL+Y
- Replace and Find Next: CTRL+H
- Scrivener Link: CTRL+G, CTRL+D
- Search in Project: CTRL+G, CTRL+S
- Select All: CTRL+A
- Show Spelling: CTRL+G
- Undo: CTRL+Z
- Use Selection for Find: CTRL+G, CTRL+F

FILE

- Close Project: CTRL+F4
- Compile: CTRL+⇧+E
- Export Files: CTRL+⇧+X
- Import Files: CTRL+⇧+J
- Import Web Page: CTRL+⇧+W
- New Project: CTRL+G, CTRL+N
- Open Project: CTRL+O
- Page Setup: CTRL+⇧+P
- Print Preview: CTRL+G, CTRL+R
- Print: CTRL+P
- Save As: CTRL+⇧+S
- Save: CTRL+S

FORMAT

- Align Center: CTRL+E
- Align Justified: CTRL+J
- Align Left: CTRL+L
- Align Right: CTRL+R
- Bold: CTRL+B
- Capitalize: CTRL+6
- Comment: ⇧+F4
- Copy Formatting: CTRL+⇧+C
- Copy Ruler: CTRL+G, CTRL+C
- Double Line Spacing: CTRL+⇧+2
- Enlarge Font: CTRL+>
- Fonts: F4
- Footnote: ⇧+F5
- Formatting: CTRL+⇧+Y
- Inline Annotation: CTRL+⇧+A
- Inline Footnote: CTRL+⇧+F
- Italic: CTRL+I
- Outlined: CTRL+;
- Paste Ruler: CTRL+G, CTRL+P
- Script Elements Popup: CTRL+\
- Script Writing: CTRL+4
- Show Citations: CTRL+G, CTRL+O
- Shrink Font: CTRL+<
- Single Half Line Spacing: CTRL+⇧+3
- Single Line Spacing: CTRL+⇧+1
- Strike Through: CTRL+⇧+-
- Sub Script: CTRL+G, CTRL+Down
- Super Script: CTRL+G, CTRL+Up
- To Single Spaces: CTRL+Space
- To Smart Quotes: CTRL+`
- To Straight Quotes: CTRL+⇧+`
- Toggle Format Bar: Meta+⇧+R
- Toggle Invisibles: CTRL+⇧+\

- Toggle Ruler: CTRL+⇧+R
- Toggle Styles Panel: CTRL+G, CTRL+E
- Toggle Typewriter Scrolling: CTRL+G, CTRL+T
- Underlined: CTRL+U

NAVIGATE

- Alternate Editor Back: CTRL+G, CTRL+[
- Alternate Editor Forward: CTRL+G, CTRL+]
- Current Editor Back: CTRL+[
- Current Editor Forward: CTRL+]
- Editor Selection: Alt+⇧+Right
- Enclosing Group: Alt+⇧+Left
- Full Screen Go To: CTRL+G, CTRL+G
- FULLSCREEN ONLY
- Next Collection: CTRL+G, CTRL+⇧+]
- Next Container: CTRL+⇧+Down
- Next Document: Alt+⇧+Down
- Previous Collection: CTRL+G, CTRL+⇧+[
- Previous Container: CTRL+⇧+Up
- Previous Document: Alt+⇧+Up
- Reveal in Binder: CTRL+⇧+8

HELP

- Scrivener Manual: F1

OTHER

- Decrease Left Indent: CTRL+⇧+M
- Decrease Text Indent: CTRL+⇧+T
- Increase Left Indent: CTRL+M

- Increase Text Indent: CTRL+T
- PROJECT
- Add New Folder: CTRL+⇧+N
- Add New from First Template: CTRL+T, CTRL+N
- Add New Text: CTRL+N
- Edit Project Settings: CTRL+⇧+CTRL+
- Project Statistics: CTRL+.
- Project Targets: CTRL+,
- Show Auto Complete List: CTRL+⇧+4
- Show Project Notes: Meta+Alt+⇧+B
- Text Statistics: CTRL+/
- Toggle Keywords HUD: CTRL+⇧+O
- TOOLS
- Collapse All to Current Level: Alt+-
- Collapse All: Alt+[
- Define in WordNet: CTRL+G, CTRL+F3
- Expand All: Alt+]
- Fast Forward Action: CTRL+}
- Focus Next Major Element: CTRL+Tab
- Horizontal Editor Split: CTRL++
- Inspector Comments and Footnotes: Meta+Alt+⇧+5
- Inspector Custom Metadata: Meta+Alt+⇧+3
- Inspector Document Bookmarks: Meta+Alt+⇧+2
- Inspector Keywords: Meta+Alt+⇧+K
- Inspector Notes: Meta+Alt+⇧+1
- Inspector Snapshots: Meta+Alt+⇧+4
- Inspector Synopsis: Meta+Alt+⇧+S
- No Editor Split: CTRL+'
- Options: CTRL+
- Rewind Action: CTRL+{
- Show Binder Tint: F5
- Show Corkboard: CTRL+2
- Show Icon Tint: F6
- Show Index Card Keywords: CTRL+F12
- Show Index Card Label: F9

- Show Index Card Status: F10
- Show Index Card Tint: F7
- Show Outliner Tint: F8
- Show Outliner: CTRL+3
- Show Text: CTRL+1
- Space bar to open selected docs as Quick Reference
- Toggle Binder: CTRL+⇧+B
- Toggle Collections: CTRL+⇧+9
- Toggle Editor Lock: CTRL+⇧+L
- Toggle Full Screen: F11
- Toggle Inspector: CTRL+⇧+I
- Toggle Page View: Meta+Alt+⇧+P
- Toggle Scratch Pad: CTRL+⇧+0
- Toggle Synopsis Text and Image: Meta+⇧+I
- Vertical Editor Split: CTRL+⇧+'

VIEW

- Zoom In: CTRL+=
- Zoom Out: CTRL+-

Now that you know about the key components of Scrivener 3 and how they work together and you know how to customize the settings in Scrivener to work best with your writing style, it's time to talk about the best practices in Scrivener 3 for saving your valuable work.

CHAPTER 4

Document Safety Protocol

Writing is tough work. It's even tougher when you have to redo it because of lost or corrupt files. Scrivener does everything in its power to make sure this doesn't happen to you. Even so, it is best to prepare for something catastrophic.

Unfortunately, I have first-hand knowledge of this. Several years ago, I had computer problems and these problems caused my software to become unstable and not work as it was supposed to. Sadly, I lost about fifteen thousand words of my work-in-progress. It was completely devastating and demoralizing.

It was also a profound learning experience. Even if you think your backup protocol is solid, it is good to build in redundancy. So, this section is about setting up Scrivener to protect your work and building in redundancy to your file management to prevent loss. Fortunately, Scrivener 3 has several tools to help protect your project from data loss.

Setting up Automatic Backup Feature

The first tool in Scrivener 3's arsenal to protect you from data loss is the Automatic Backup Feature.

You can set up this feature from the Options menu (CTRL+) by selecting the Backup option.

FIGURE 43: Setting up Automatic Backup Feature for Scrivener 3 in Preferences

If you have the hard drive space, I recommend keeping the greatest number of recent backups. Since I use an external drive to back up my entire hard drive several times a day, I could back up my files on my actual hard drive. However, if you don't back up your files externally on a regular basis, you might want to choose a location on the cloud. I have chosen to back up my projects upon closing them. However, you can choose different options if you wish.

Cloud services, which may not play well with Scrivener 3 when working with live files, for your work-in-progress will function just fine for saving your backup files since they are zipped.

You can also manually back up your files. To do this, you can click on File ▸ Backup. Optionally, you can add an icon to your toolbar.

The Automatic Backup Feature is not the only protection you have for your files. Next, we'll discuss the role of Snapshot in protecting your data.

Snapshots

The Snapshot feature is just what it sounds like. It allows you to take a picture of a moment in time of your folders and documents. As a subtle reminder to myself to use this feature more often, I have placed it in my toolbar. However, if you have not done so, you can access this feature through the document menu. If you want to save a Snapshot with a title, the keyboard shortcut is CTRL ⇧5. If you don't wish to include a title, the keyboard shortcut is CTRL 5. Personally, I find it helpful to add a title so I know what I'm looking at later. I will often note the changes I have made in a particular Snapshot. It is a good idea to take a Snapshot every time you make substantial changes to your document.

Honestly, I don't use the Snapshot feature as often as I should. Because this feature differs from the software I grew up using, I forget the feature is there. However, it is very helpful when you are making edits because you can compare the differences in Snapshot. The Snapshot feature allows you to roll back your folder or document to a previous version if you don't like the changes you've made. If your file has a Snapshot attached to it, it will have a special indicator on the folder or document. The corner of the document in the folder will be folded down.

To work with your Snapshot, look for the camera icon in the Inspector. If you have a Snapshot in a folder, a little dot will appear above the camera in the Inspector. The date and title of your Snapshot will appear in the menu. You can compare Snapshots or roll back your document to a previous version.

By using the Snapshot manager, you can compare Snapshots by phrase or paragraph and export your Snapshot to another kind of file. Documents ▸ Snapshot ▸ Snapshot Manager. To export your Snapshot, click on the gear in the bottom left-hand corner.

If you are syncing with the iOS version, turn on the feature which will take a Snapshot when you update your file. To do this, click on preferences and then sharing. Under the sync tab, there are several options for syncing your files—including one to take a Snapshot.

In addition to working with the Automatic Backup feature and Snapshot, you can also save your files to your Dropbox. In the next section, I will discuss Dropbox and other cloud services.

FIGURE 44: Settings to Automatically Take a Snapshot when Syncing Your Files

Saving to the Cloud

For your own peace of mind, you may use a cloud service to save your Scrivener files. This option is helpful if you are using Scrivener on several computers.

If you are using the iOS version of Scrivener together with the Windows version, you'll need Dropbox to sync your files.

If you don't backup your hard drive to an external device, you might consider saving your backup copies of Scrivener files to a cloud service.

Regardless of which cloud service you choose, make sure you wait until your file is fully saved before you close Scrivener. Failing to do so can cause corruption in your file.

Dropbox

If you use a cloud service to save your files as you work with them, Literature and Latte recommends Dropbox. Dropbox has recently updated its paid service to include a rollback feature if something catastrophic has occurred to your current file.

If you use Dropbox, it is critically important that you allow the project to completely finish saving before you close Scrivener.

Scrivener 3 for Windows works well with Dropbox and makes switching back and forth between the Windows version and iOS easy. Just make sure you save the file in an area the iOS program can locate. To sync files between platforms, the default path to save your project looks like this:

Dropbox ▸ apps ▸ Scrivener ▸ [project name]

OneDrive

Although OneDrive is a popular cloud service, it is not particularly stable when using it with live files in Scrivener 3 because of the way files are saved in Scrivener. Therefore, if you use OneDrive, use it as a supplemental location to save your backup files within Scrivener. I don't recommend using OneDrive as your primary save location for your projects.

There are anecdotal reports of people using OneDrive successfully, however there are many more reports of negative experiences with OneDrive.

Google Drive

Again, Google Drive is a helpful location for your backup files. However, I don't recommend using Google Drive as your primary save location for Scrivener because of Google Drive's tendency to convert files. Backup files are saved as zip files and Google Drive doesn't convert those files as they do other types of files used in saving live projects in Scrivener.

It is a good idea to back up your Scrivener files to the cloud. However, that's not the only thing you need to save to an external location. In the next section we will talk about other files, key to the success of Scrivener, that you need to export and save.

Other Things to Backup

This is one of those lessons I learned the hard way.

Just because your projects are backed up, it doesn't mean all your favorite settings in Scrivener are saved.

During a catastrophic failure of my computer, I discovered that backing up your preferences, section layouts, themes and formats is also important. If you fail to do this, you will have to rebuild your favorite settings. I am including this advice to save you from the mistakes I've made.

First, once you have made all the changes under the Options menu (CTRL+), click on Manage and save your preferences to an external file. In Scrivener 3 for Windows, this option is called Save Options to File. It will create a file with a .Prefs extension. Therefore, if you work with both the Mac and Windows version of Scrivener 3, you should put the operating system in the title of your preferences when you save them.

When you save a theme using Save Theme to File, you will need to choose a name. If you use multiple operating systems, you may want to include the name of your operating system in your theme. I recommend saving these files in the cloud or on a thumb drive, so they are easily retrievable in the event of a catastrophe.

There are other things which need to be exported and saved as well. You can save Section Types by right clicking on a file in your Binder and clicking on Section Types and going down to the bottom of the menu and clicking on edit. After you've done that, click on Section Types and export.

Unfortunately, status and label features don't have the same import and export ability. However, you can highlight the status or label types you want to use in another project and drag them over to the new project.

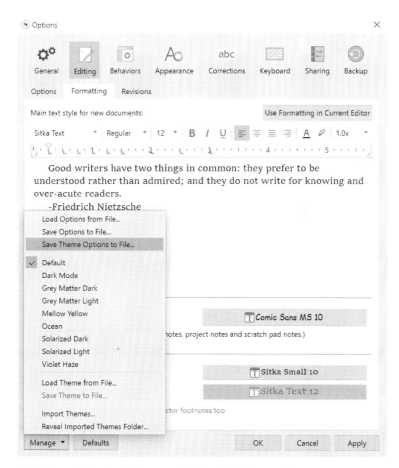

FIGURE 45: Saving Themes to File in Scrivener 3

Under compile, you can export your formats in either Scrivener 3 or Scrivener 2 formats if you need a backward compatibility.

(Although Scrivener 3 for Windows is compatible with files created with Scrivener 3 for Mac, if you want to work with older versions of Scrivener, you must work with your project as a Scrivener 2 project.)

Now that you've learned how to back up your project and settings, I'd like to talk about some best practices for ensuring your work against catastrophe that I've discovered the hard way.

Best Practices

As I mentioned before, nothing teaches you the really hard lessons like a catastrophic computer failure. After I lost fifteen thousand words, I became much more diligent about my redundancy and file management. I know some of this might seem extreme, but peace of mind is worth a lot.

After I had my catastrophic data loss, I discovered the value of backing up your files to an external drive. I have the benefit of using Time Machine on my MacBook Pro to automatically backup both my data and my applications seamlessly in the background.

However, if you are operating on a Windows computer without the benefit of using Parallels, *PC Magazine* identifies Genie Timeline and Macrium Reflect as comprehensive programs which back up both your data and your programs on the Windows platform.

In addition to Time Machine, I save all my Scrivener files in my Dropbox account. To me, it is worth the nominal fee to back my files up on the cloud. Of all the cloud services which allow you to save live files of your work-in-progress, Dropbox is the most compatible with Scrivener.

If you wish, you can also use programs like Carbonite to give yourself another layer of protection.

Because I don't want to deal with the consequences of major data loss again, I take some additional steps. Whether you will be as fastidious about backing up your Scrivener projects or not is up to you.

Every few months, I save all of my Scrivener files onto a thumb drive in addition to using Time Machine and Dropbox. I can't repeat this often enough.

When you are saving your files, make sure your computer is done with the process before you close Scrivener. If you don't do this, it can corrupt your files.

I have gotten into the habit of compiling my Scrivener project every day or so and sending myself a copy of my Word document via Facebook. If you don't want to use Facebook, you can also just email yourself a copy. Although restoring from a Word document would take some time, having a Word document is better than having no copy of your work-in-progress. I have spoken to several authors who have had their laptops stolen or destroyed and as a result, they lost all of their writing. It is a heartbreaking scenario to consider. It might be worth the extra step in case the worst happens.

Now that we have discussed the parts of Scrivener, their function, and how to safely protect your words, let's talk about working with your manuscript in Scrivener.

CHAPTER 5

Working with a Manuscript

When I started working with Scrivener, I was in the middle of a project. It was no problem because Scrivener 3 is flexible. Not only can you start a project from scratch in Scrivener, you can also easily import an existing manuscript written in another application.

In this chapter, I'll discuss ways to start a manuscript, import a manuscript and apply different formatting tools like styles, labels, Section Types and special formatting.

Let's begin with starting a manuscript from scratch.

Starting from Scratch

I have touched on this briefly, but you can easily start a document from scratch in Scrivener 3. If the project template window does not open for you, press CTRL G, CTRL N or choose new project under the file menu.

You will be presented with a variety of templates available by default from Scrivener or any templates you have imported.

To start a new project, simply choose the template that's closest to what you would like to accomplish. However, if you want the features from another type of template, you can add those files to your project by creating a project with the alternative template and dragging the folders over to the Binder of your work in progress.

Don't worry about choosing exactly the right template. The contents of your Binder can always be adjusted and expanded. For example, if you choose a short story template and your work-in-progress ends up being a novel, you can always add more folders to your Binder.

You will be asked to save your project immediately.

If you later change your mind and want to call your project something else, it's very easy to change it with the rename function in Windows Explorer. Just make sure you close your Scrivener project first.

Scrivener 3 has added a handy feature to the file menu called Favorite Projects. If the project you have created is one you plan to access frequently, you may want to add your project to this list. Unlike recent documents, this list stays constant regardless of how many other files you have opened. To add a file to this list, choose File ▸ Add Project to Favorites. This feature will sort your projects alphabetically to make them easier to find when you have several.

Once you have created your project, you will have a Binder on the left-hand side of the page. You can write directly into

Scrivener by choosing the Document or Scrivenings mode. Most of your manuscript needs to go in the Draft Folder. Your front and back matter are the exception to this rule. They go in the Research Folder. As mentioned before, the other two mandatory folders are the Research and Trash Folders. If you have extraneous material such as pictures, charts, audio clips, video clips or Excel files, they can all go in the Research Folder.

You can add additional folders and scenes to the Draft Folder. To add a folder press CTRL ⇧ N. If you want a document, use CTRL N. You can also right-click on any folder or in your binder and choose Add Folder or Text. If you set a default template, you can also add a folder from a template. To set up your default template, go to Project ▸ Project Settings ▸ Special Folders.

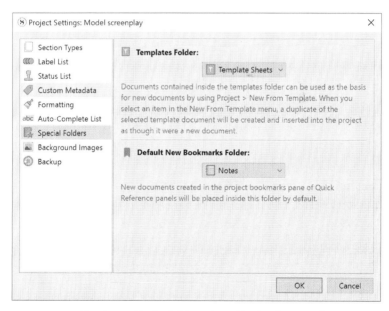

FIGURE 46: Setting a Default Template Under Project Settings in Scrivener 3 for Windows

Alternatively, if you like to plan your work before you start to write, you can use the corkboard or outline view.

Personally, I prefer to set up my page parameters in page set up under the file menu. (CTRL⇧P) Although I do finish formatting using Microsoft Word when I am finished with my manuscript, choosing the page size and margins gives me a rough idea of how my project flows on the page when I use the page view settings. To access the page view, go to View ▸ Text Editing ▸ Page View.

You may be thinking to yourself, that's fine if I'm starting from scratch. However, I already have a manuscript started in another program like Microsoft Word. That's okay, Scrivener has a mechanism for importing files from other applications. We will discuss that next.

Importing Work Done in Other Applications

Scrivener has two primary ways to import documents created in other applications. The first is a straight import function. I rarely use this type of import because I prefer Scrivener's more functional alternative: Import and Split. Import and Split allows you to mark up a copy of your original document and then import it into chapters.

First, I'll talk about the simple import procedure, then I will move on to Import and Split.

Import

It is possible to import files directly into Scrivener using File ▸ Import ▸ Files. Scrivener 3 can import your files from

Microsoft Word, OpenOffice or RTF. These files can be stored in your Draft Folder—just make sure your Draft Folder (or a sub-folder you've created) is clicked in your Binder before you import.

Make sure you know where your document is located. I don't typically use this feature much because I have written in Scrivener for nearly five years. So, when I was experimenting with this option, I inadvertently tried to import a very large file with over three thousand documents in it. Fortunately, I was able to cancel the transfer before much damage was done. Even if the files had been transferred to my Binder or Research Folder, I could easily move them to the trash.

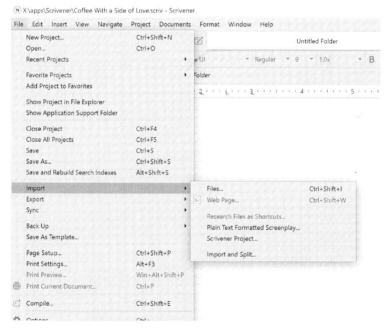

FIGURE 47: Importing Files, Screenplays or Scrivener Projects in Scrivener 3 For Windows

If you import images or websites into your Binder, you need to place them in your Research Folder. However, if you need to use images in your project, there is a different procedure to accomplish that. I will discuss using images in your project in Chapter 9.

If your document is in PDF form or was created in Pages, you will need to convert it to a Word or RTF document first. The same is true for .EPUB and .MOBI files.

It is possible to import files from an existing Scrivener project or a screenplay formatted with plain text from this menu.

Although it is relatively painless to import files into Scrivener, sometimes a file may arrive as one big block of text. Fortunately, Scrivener has an answer to this problem. The solution is called Import and Split.

Import and Split

The Import and Split feature was one of the first tools I ever used in Scrivener. I suspect that might be true for many of you too. This tool is very useful if you have created a document in another application which you need broken down into the proper folders in your Binder.

To use the Import and Split function, I recommend you create a working copy of your Microsoft Word document (just for safekeeping).

The next step in the process involves giving Scrivener some cues about where you would like the splits to occur in your pre-existing document. Personally, I like to use $&$ as my markers because that combination of characters is not likely to appear in my document naturally.

Open the working document you created. Every place you want to separate into a folder such as your dedication, copyright or forward as well as every chapter (and scene, if you wish), you need to place the symbols to alert Scrivener 3 of your intent.

You can do this function with a global search and replace. Which symbol you use depends upon how you've constructed your Microsoft Word document. Some people use page breaks. In search and replace, this symbol is ^m. Other authors prefer to use section breaks. In Microsoft Word, this is represented by ^b. If you use section breaks instead of page breaks, you must do one more step of preparation. To make the process smoother (because of Microsoft Word's limitations on Find and Replace), you should do a global find and replace substitute page breaks for section breaks. To prepare your document for Import and Split if you have used section breaks, you would type the following:

Find: ^b
Replace with: ^m

After you have page breaks, then do the following search and replace function:

Find: ^m
Replace with: $&$ ^m

This function places $&$ at the end of each section of your document. This will enable Scrivener 3 to split your document into individual folders when you import.

To start the process of Import and Split, go to File ‣ Import ‣ Import and Split. Then choose the working file you created under Browse.

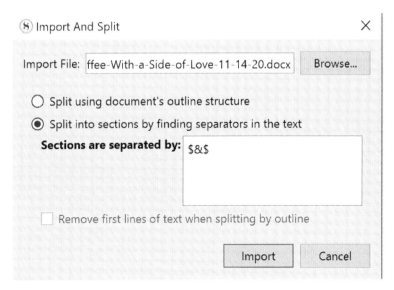

FIGURE 48: Import and Split Menu in Scrivener 3

You'll note that the special symbols we placed in our working document are in the window which determines how the sections are separated. You can change the symbols to anything you wish. Just make sure they are consistent between your working document and the Import and Split window.

Then, click on import. It is important to pay attention to what is selected in your Binder before you click import. The first few times I tried to use this tool; I was not cognizant of this factor. Sometimes, my imported document landed in the Trash Folder. If that happens to you, you can just drag it up to your Draft Folder.

Magic will happen—yes, I know it's actually computer programming—but it seems like magic when your document appears in the Binder pre-sorted into documents. If you prefer to work in folders rather than documents, you can highlight the document in your Binder and right-click on it. This will give you an option to convert your documents to folders.

Doing a global search and replace works really well if your original document has labels on each section. Sometimes you

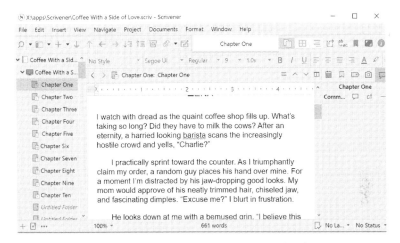

FIGURE 49: Documents Created by Import and Split

may work with a document with no such titles. In that case, Scrivener will display the first eight or nine words in each section as the title of the document.

If your working document does not have titles before each section, you can either change the name of each imported document in your Binder or you can add a title below each separator in your working document before you perform the import. This is my preferred method if I'm trying to assign chapters to a block of text.

If you want to choose each folder individually, you can press CTRL as you choose multiple folders.

If you want to select multiple folders in your Binder, you can press the ⇧ to choose the first and last folder and everything in between will be selected. Or, if you want to choose each folder individually, you can press CTRL as you choose multiple folders.

Sometimes we authors change our mind about where scenes should go or how they are arranged. That's okay, Scrivener has you covered with the Split and Merge functions. You can adjust your document on the fly without having to copy and paste. We will talk about this handy tool next.

Split and Merge

One of the handiest features in Scrivener 3 is its ability to split and merge documents without having to copy and paste. I use this feature most often when I am editing, and I realize that I needed to add a section break because the action takes place in a different time frame or location.

Before I discovered Scrivener, I used to manually divide my scenes through copy and paste. Now, if I want to split a scene into two, I can place my cursor before the first word of the part I want in a different folder and click on Document ▸ Split.

Scrivener 3 will add the second portion of your document to a new file. So, if your scene was called Scene 2, the new file will be Scene 2-1. The synopsis, notes and comments will remain with the first file. If you need them in both, you must copy and paste the information into your new file.

When using the split feature, you can place words at the beginning of the area you want to split off and select them. These words will become the title of your new folder.

If you got a little too ambitious with your scene dividing or you simply decide the smaller scenes work better as one larger scene. No problem. It's an easy fix with Scrivener 3.

Highlight the folders you want to merge in your Binder. Then click on Document ▸ Merge or use CTRL G, CTRL M on your keyboard. Your files or documents will be combined into the top file or document you clicked. The Metadata from the documents will be combined.

You also have the option to select a chunk of text and have Scrivener place it in a new file for you. This function is found under Documents ▸ New Folder from Selection or you can press CTRL G, CTRL U.

Sometimes, you may need to export a file from Scrivener. We'll talk about that next.

Export

I don't use the export feature of Scrivener often. However, it is useful for a couple of things. First, if you are working with a Scrivener project with teammates, you can export your Scrivener project in a variety of different formats.

You can choose to include your notes, annotations and comments as well as number your exported files. Generally speaking, a compiled document will be easier to manage, but some people choose to use this feature if they don't want to mess with the parameters in Compile.

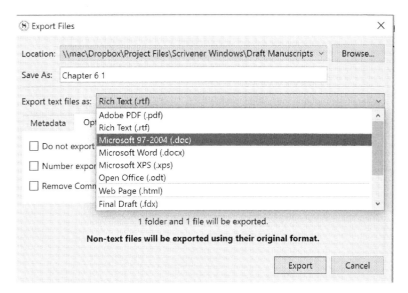

FIGURE 50: Exporting Files in Scrivener 3 For Windows

The other cool thing you can export are your comments and in-line annotations. Many authors like to use the comment feature to keep running notes to themselves or to assist with editing. In-line annotations can work the same way. In fact, you can color code them to show point of view, progression along a timeline or virtually anything else. You can even drag a picture of your character into the comments or annotations if you need a quick reference. Scrivener makes it possible for you to export all these comments and annotations.

To export your annotations, click on File ▸ Export ▸ Comments and Annotations. A menu will appear that can limit the export to just the current selected file (among other things).

You can also use drag and drop files directly on the binder. This feature works best when working with other Scrivener 3 files because of the limited number of file types which respond to this method of moving files.

Sync

The sync function is another option I don't use often. I prefer to use Compile instead for most functions. However, there are a couple of situations in which the Sync function might be helpful. To reach the Sync menu, click on File ▸ Sync.

First, there is an option to sync to mobile devices. Selecting this option will force Scrivener to check against your mobile devices to determine whether your project needs to be updated. According to Literature and Latte, you should not have to use this feature to work with the iOS version of Scrivener. However, if you are uncertain whether your file has properly synced, it isn't harmful to use this function.

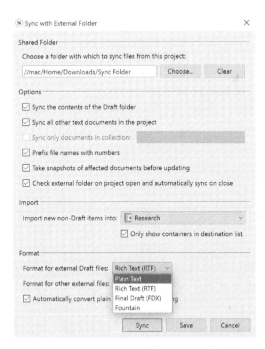

FIGURE 51: Syncing with External Folder in Scrivener 3 for Windows

Additionally, you can sync text or RTF files to external folders. This might be a helpful feature if you are working in collaboration with someone else. For example, you can import the text files into Google docs. If you are a screenwriter, there is an option to export the files in a format compatible with Final Draft. You can elect to sync your entire Draft Folder or individual parts.

Do not use the sync with External Folder function to update your files in the IOS version of Scrivener.

Styles

Styles are new in Scrivener 3. However, if you have used earlier versions of Scrivener, you are likely familiar with the features included in Styles. Styles are just a name for a group of formatting characteristics which you can save for later use. Personally, I am a big fan of the Styles function because it allows me to have consistent formatting throughout my entire series.

The older version Scrivener had Formatting Presets, but that feature was not as robust as the new Styles feature.

Scrivener 3 allows you to assign fonts, colors, spacing and indents to a style. If you change a style in Scrivener 3, the changes are automatically applied to all the text which has been assigned to that particular title. This feature is helpful if you decide to change your formatting midway through a project.

Scrivener 3 comes with some Styles already defined. They are located on your format bar and include things like headings, title, attribution, and block quotes. If you choose No Style, your document is formatted according to the default settings under preferences.

If you choose block quote as a style, it won't be justified on both sides because of a limitation in Scrivener. It will, however, be indented.

If none of Scrivener 3's preset Styles meet your needs, you can add your own. There are several ways to accomplish this. You can adapt an existing style with your own font color or spacing choices. After you have made the appropriate changes to the text, simply highlight the text that is representative of what you want your Style to be and add it to the list of Styles. To do this, you can click on the Show Styles Panel which is at the end of the menu of your existing styles. Then just click the plus sign and a menu will appear which looks like this:

Most of the time when I add a new Style, I don't save all the formatting. I select Save Paragraph Style instead. I've learned the hard way that saving all the formatting can wipe out existing italics or bold formatting. Here, I want the style to include bold and italics, so I chose to save all the formatting. Personally, I don't use a lot of keyboard shortcuts because of my mobility limitations. However, you can assign keyboard

FIGURE 52: Adding a New Style to Scrivener 3

123

shortcuts to individual styles. If you are working with a lot of different styles in a single document, you may have the styles highlighted in a particular color.

I feel the need to make a small confession here. I set up the style to make my photo captions in Scrivener 3. Later, I went back to add a highlight box to my style so I could tell when I applied it. Unfortunately, when I did that, I inadvertently selected the picture too. Therefore, when I applied my style the next time, it replaced my graphic with the one I have included in the style. Fortunately, I discovered this right away or it could have resulted in a long reedit. So, after I discovered my mistake, I selected the proper portion of my caption and then went to Format ▸ Style ▸ Redefine Style from Selection. This brings up a menu for you to select your choices. This time, I chose save paragraph style and added a highlight box.

You can also assign a style type to existing text. This is my favorite way to create styles. I simply open a file which contains text that is formatted the way I prefer and then I go to Format ▸ Style ▸ New style from Selection. This sequence brings up the same menu as above. You can keep all formatting, paragraph formatting or character formatting.

Remember we talked about indents on the ruler tool before? I use New Style from Selection to create a non-indented version of my existing styles. I use these styles after a section break or for the first paragraph of my chapter. To create this, I use a paragraph that's already formatted to my liking. If that paragraph is already indented, I drag the indent on the ruler so that the beginning of my text is lined up with the rest of the paragraph. Then, I save the non-indented paragraph as a style all of its own. For example, I have *Garamond Indented* and *Garamond No Indent*.

Ironically, there is no mechanism to export your styles. However, you can import them from one project to another. To do so, simply open the show styles panel at the bottom of your style list and click on the gear. After you've done that, import styles is at the bottom of the list. It will direct you to open a Scrivener file. Just choose the Scrivener file which has the styles you wish to transfer to your new project.

In addition to styles, you may work with labels in your project.

Labels

Labels are exactly what they sound like. They are a mechanism to add more information to your project. You can have the labels show up in your section formatting.

Although in some sections of my manuscript, I use the label function in my chapter headings, you don't have to. You can use labels to track all types of things from point of view, to the progress you've made in your manuscript. In fact, the way I use labels changes during the progress of writing a book.

Since I frequently work on more than one project at once, I change the label color for my characters, so it is easy for me to tell at a glance which file I'm working on. Then, when I get to the editing process, I change the label colors to show what I need to work on. For example, if I need to add more detail about a couple's relationship, I change the color of the label to bright yellow to remind me to go back into that particular file and adjust the content. I do the same thing for location details or pacing issues. Using labels allows me to continue editing while marking potential issues with my manuscript. If your story takes place in different time periods, you can use labels to remind you to anchor your scenes on a timeline.

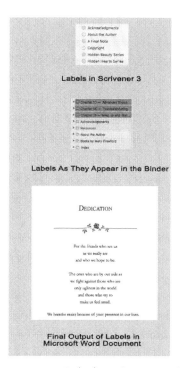

FIGURE 53: Labels in Scrivener 3

If you change your labels during the editing process and you use them in your compile settings, make sure you change them back before you compile.

Labels are easy to use. To get started, you can add a label by clicking on the footer bar status under the Inspector. Alternatively, you can right-click on the document or file in your Binder to attach a label. If you want to edit the labels, scroll down to the individual list and click on Edit. You can change both the text and the color.

If the labels don't appear in your Binder, there is an option under View to change the way labels appear. You can include them in your Binder, your outline or your index cards on your corkboard. In Scrivener 3, you can either display the label colors as a dot next to your text or you can have the label color show as a background color across your Binder.

Labels are a simple way to add information in context to your folders or documents in Scrivener. In the next section, I'll discuss a more complex feature new to Scrivener 3: Section Type.

Section Type

The introduction of the Section Types is one of the most visible changes in Scrivener 3. Personally, I think it's also one of the most helpful. In previous editions of Scrivener, it was difficult to visualize formatting changes as you applied them. The introduction of Section Types changes all that.

One concept that was foreign to me when I started using Scrivener was the idea that it didn't matter how I set up Scrivener during the writing process, compiling could change everything without impacting my manuscript in the Binder. Once you realize that these processes are largely separate, it is easier to understand the compile function.

The first step in using the new compile set up is to assign Section Types. This is not the same as assigning Styles to change the way your project appears on the screen. Assigning Section Types just categorizes different types of content in your Binder. For example, the following are Section Types I use when writing my romance novels.

There are several ways to assign Section Types. First, as shown above, you can click on the Metadata tab in your Inspector and

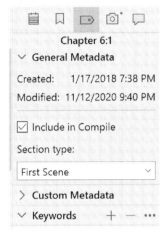

FIGURE 54: Section Layout Indicators in Scrivener 3

assign each file or document its own Section Type. Additionally, you can right-click on a folder or document in your Binder and assign it that way. You can highlight several folders or documents by pressing CTRL while you click on folders or documents. You can then assign Section Types in bulk. If you are a fan of outlining, you can have Section Type show in your outline and adjust your Section Types there.

Section Types can also be assigned in the Compile Window. When you check the box to include a folder in compile, just click on the down arrow to bring up your menu of Section Types. Another cool feature of the compile menu is its ability to show you which Section Types are applied to each document.

In the following example, I have selected first scene in the Section Layout window. The compiler automatically highlights all the files in my document which are assigned to the first scene Section Type.

I created a special first scene format because I format several words of each first section in small caps.

There is one more slightly complex way of assigning section layouts in bulk. To reach this window, click on project settings under project. Then, click on Section Types ▸ Default Types by Structure.

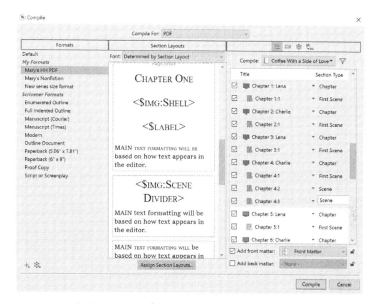

FIGURE 55: An Example of Customized Section Types in Scrivener 3

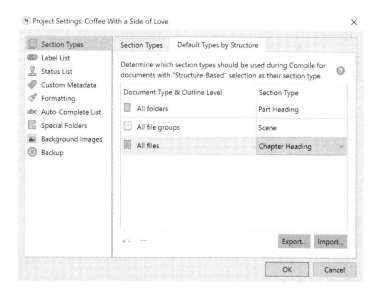

FIGURE 56: Adding Section Types by Structure

Clicking on default type by structure allows you to assign different Section Types based on the level your files appear in your Binder. For example, in the above illustration, every file that is in Level 2 or deeper, will be automatically assigned to the Titled Section section type.

Although assigning Section Types by structure is a quick way to assign section types, I often have to adjust the section types after doing this because I have multiple section types within the same level of hierarchy. For example, I have a different section type for the first scenes in the chapter and subsequent scenes. So, if I assign section types by structure, I have to go back and manually fix the files on the same level of hierarchy.

If you have a template or a file you use as a template, you can assign Section Types to your template and they will be saved across projects created with those templates.

You may be thinking to yourself, "Okay, I've assigned section layouts, but now what?"

This is the part of the process that's difficult to put into words for people who have never used Scrivener before. I will try to describe the process in simple terms.

When your document is in the Binder in Scrivener, it is somewhat analogous to a draft document. It's not a direct correlation because before Scrivener 3 arrived, I used to format my work in the Scrivenings pane exactly how I wanted it to appear in the final document and chose the as-is option when compiling. You can still do this but working with section layouts is much more straightforward, and if you use graphics as scene separators, you can save yourself on delivery service fees by automating the process with section layouts. Under some royalty structures, Amazon charges a fee to deliver your file to readers. This fee is based on file size. I used to insert each section graphic separately, but after I started automating the process by using styles, I was able to dramatically reduce my finished file size.

Anyway, if you envision the work in your Binder as a rough draft that still needs to go to the formatter or typesetter, it helps explain the role of the compiler and section layout.

When you open the compile menu, you will be presented with three panes. On the left-hand side is the format pane. Think of these as the options the printer or formatter offer. (You can customize these, and I will discuss that under Demystifying the Compiler in Chapter 12.)

The type of formats offered depends on the output you want.

For example, they are different for an e-book than they are for a Word document.

In the middle section is a list of your section layouts. This section tells the formatter how you want each part of your document handled.

On the right-hand side, is where you tell the formatter which parts of your manuscript you would like to be included in your final output.

To select all the files or documents at once, press the ALT key while you click in one of the check boxes. If you have forgotten

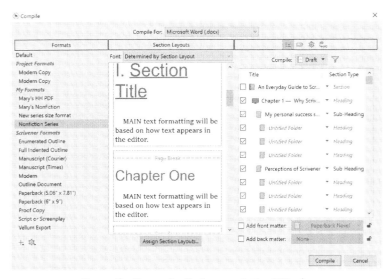

FIGURE 57: Compile Panes in Scrivener 3 For Windows

to select a Section Type for your document, you can add it from this window in compile.

Once you have selected the files from your Binder that you want to appear in your output and assign each folder or document, you can click Option and Compile. This will save the configuration for later use.

To compile the manuscript into a formatted document, first, you need to choose an output format. The Compile feature has dozens of options. I usually use two of these options for my writing, but your choices may be different. I either compile to an .EPUB or a Microsoft Word document. Although you can save your file as a .MOBI file, I don't bother anymore. I just upload an .EPUB when I post my e-books to Amazon.

On the left-hand side of the compile window is the format pane. Scrivener has a list of default formats available. These options will change depending on your output. For example, if you are outputting to a text document, your formatting options are limited.

In our analogy, this formatting option is like choosing a style for your formatter or typesetter to follow. For example, for my fiction, I have created chapter headings with specific graphics for each series and I format the first few words of each first scene with small caps. These custom touches are determined by each format. If you need to adjust the default formats, you can right-click on a format and click duplicate and save. Formats can either be attached to each project or be saved as globally available within Scrivener.

The middle section of the Compile Window is where you assign your Section Types to the format you have chosen. This is like telling your formatter how to treat each element of your manuscript. In Scrivener 3, the first time you use a format for each type of output, you will need to assign your Section Types. After that, Scrivener 3 will remember your choices for the next time you compile.

I hope this overview of the role of Section Types in the new compile system helps clarify things. I will be discussing the Compiler in more detail in Chapter 12.

Formatting

There are some random remarks I want to make about formatting.

First, under the Format menu, there is an option to format lists. This can be handy. However, remember your lists may look different when they are rendered on an e-book device because each reader has the opportunity to set their own font and spacing.

It is important to remember e-book and paperback formats need to be handled differently. Unlike paperbacks, e-book readers have the option to change the way fonts appear. E-book readers have a limited number of fonts available. If you have your heart set on a particular font for chapter headings or pullout quotes in your book and you want them to remain consistent in the e-book format, you'll need to save your font as a .JPEG or .PNG file.

Here is an example from an old version of one of my books. Incidentally, this is also the way I format my title pages which are a little on the fancy side.

As pretty as these graphics are, there are some inherent downsides. First, including graphics like this increases your delivery cost (if you choose the 70% royalty option on Amazon).

Another consideration is accessibility. Many people rely on screen readers and graphics do not translate well. One way to minimize this downside is to supply alternative descriptions for your graphics.

There is another interesting feature of formatting within Scrivener. Your font choices and compile can be easily overridden. For example, if you are submitting your manuscript to an anthology and the curators of the anthology expect your document in Times New Roman and that is not typically what you use, you can override the styles to include Times New Roman.

This setting is located above the Section Layout Pane of the Compile Window. There is a drop-down menu which says Font: If you assign a font here, it will override your Section Layout options.

I always have to search for this feature when I need it. So, I will highlight it here. If you need to change your text to superscript or subscript (as in the word 2nd

FIGURE 58: Chapter Heading Formatted in Photoshop

you can change the alignment under Format ▸ Font ▸ Baseline (CTRL G, CTRL⇧). It is important to note that when you are finished using alternative formatting, you need to go back to the menu and choose Use Default.

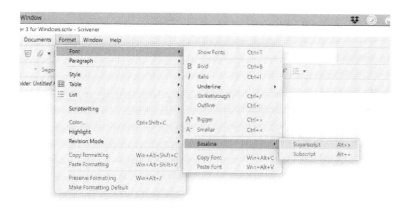

FIGURE 59: Changing Text Alignment in Scrivener 3

Additionally, choosing Paragraph from the Format menu allows you to choose many options including alignment, text direction and keeping your paragraphs together.

One last note about formatting. Scrivener 3 has an option to Preserve Formatting under the Format menu. To use this feature, select the text you want to maintain special formatting—like for example if you changed the font to something fancy. Then click on Format ▸ Preserve Formatting. It will put a highlight box around the text you have selected. The purpose of this is to keep the special formatting visible in your output. Unfortunately, this only works some of the time. It typically works in Word documents and PDFs. However, it does not work when you are creating e-books. Additionally, make sure you can embed whatever font you choose to use. Otherwise, this feature won't work.

Now that we've talked about how to work with your manuscript, let's discuss some special tools available in Scrivener 3 for Windows to make writing easier.

Revision Mode

Although it is not exactly the same as track changes in Microsoft Word, you can keep track of your revisions in Scrivener.

To use this tool, go to Format ▸ Revision Mode. After you have entered into this mode, you can assign a color to the changes you've made. You can change the colors available in the revision mode; however, there doesn't seem to be a way to change the name of each mode. You may want to add a comment at the beginning of your manuscript which includes the key to your revision tasks. For example, you could make all points of view revisions a particular color and punctuation a different color, if you wish. Or, you can just make different rounds of revisions. Unlike text changes in Microsoft Word, using the revisions mode does not actually change your manuscript. It just allows you to keep track of your revisions.

Another way to track revisions is through in-line annotations. There is a setting in Compile that allows you to disregard any comments and annotations in your final product.

Scrivener will continue to add text in a separate color until you exit from revision mode. To exit from revision mode, click Remove Current Revision Color. Clicking on Remove All Revisions restores the text to its original color.

Revision mode does not make corrections. It just helps you identify where they need to be made.

Speech to Text and Text to Speech

If you have the accessibility features turned on through your Window's operating system, you can use the speech to text capability in Scrivener 3 to dictate your documents.

The speech to text engine included for free in the operating system of Windows is not as accurate as an external program like Dragon Professional Individual 15.3. However, it is a usable program. Be aware it does not learn custom vocabulary words or learn from its mistakes. Even so, it can be a valuable tool (and it's free).

To access the speech to text capabilities within Scrivener, press the Windows Key + H

In a related function, you can have Scrivener read your text back to you. To set it up, go to Edit ▸ Speech ▸ Settings. You can choose the pitch, speed and voice the computer uses to read back your document.

Although it might sound a little funny, it is a very helpful tool to catch punctuation and grammar errors in your manuscript. To start the text-to-speech function, go to Edit ▸ Speech ▸ Start. To stop the computer from reading your text, use Edit ▸ Speech ▸ Stop.

Now that we've discussed working with a manuscript in Scrivener 3; in the next chapter, I will talk about some tools built into Scrivener 3 that will make producing a quality manuscript a little easier.

CHAPTER 6

Tools to Improve
Your Manuscript

I t's hard to identify all the helpful peripheral features in
Scrivener 3 for Windows because they are wide and varied.
I'll address a few of them here. I acknowledge, this is not
an exhaustive list. It is just a few of the features I use most often.

Collections

Scrivener has many tools to assist your writing process.

The Collections feature is just one of them. This tool is great
for determining internal consistency within your manuscript.
For example, you may want to make a collection of chapters
which follow a particular character to make sure the details are
consistent all the way through your manuscript. You could also
make collections from the chapters you've already finished and
the chapters you still have to work on. Collections can be made
up of any variable you would like to include. If your project

contains any collections, you can have them appear above your Binder by clicking the blue view button in the left-hand corner of your toolbar.

You can use tags you have added to your work such as labels, status or keywords to build your collections. To add files based on a search of these terms, you can bring up the search tool by using CTRL F. Click on the magnifying glass and a list of options will appear. After your search results are created, you can click on the magnifying glass again and choose Save Search as a Collection. Collections based on search results have a magnifying glass in front of the title. You can click the arrow next to the X and generate all the documents in the search in an editor window. You can work with collections in any of the group modes, including Scrivenings, Corkboard and Outline. If you add more files which meet the criteria of the search, just push this button again and it will be updated.

You can also create a collection by manually adding documents or files to a Collection. A manually created Collection has a solid background instead of a striped one. To create one, use the CTRL key as you click on folders and documents you want to include. When you are finished, press the + next to the Collections window. This will create a collection called new collection. If you want to change the title of this Collection, click on it and type a new word. You can add and subtract files from this Collection by dragging files into the Collection and clicking the minus key to remove them.

After you are done working with your Collections, you can hide the Collections view by clicking on the blue view button in your toolbar.

Spell Check

Scrivener offers a spellcheck tool. To access it, you can add an icon when you customize the toolbar or right-click on a word in your document. The spell check tool is an option on the menu that appears. Alternatively, you can also press CTRL G, CTRL Q to start the spellcheck immediately. The spellcheck feature underlines misspelled words.

I'll be honest with you; I have a love/hate relationship with the spell checker in Scrivener. In many ways, it is helpful. The tool can help you identify spelling errors. However, like many other tools to check spelling, the advice you receive can be incorrect. There are certain words it has a difficult time sorting through, including there and it's. Additionally, there is a tool tip which is supposed to appear when you click on an underlined word. However, it never seems to work properly for me. I must not have the magic touch with my mouse.

I vastly prefer an external program called ProWritingAid (which incidentally works with Scrivener projects) because it offers both spelling and a comprehensive grammar check. I still use the spell checker to help me clean up my writing as I draft my manuscript before I start my formal edit.

You can easily add words to the spell checker by clicking on a misspelled word and telling the spellchecker to learn a word. These settings are easily accessible under File ▸ Options ▸ Corrections. If you need to eliminate a word you have added to the spell-checker, edit your word list. You can also add words here.

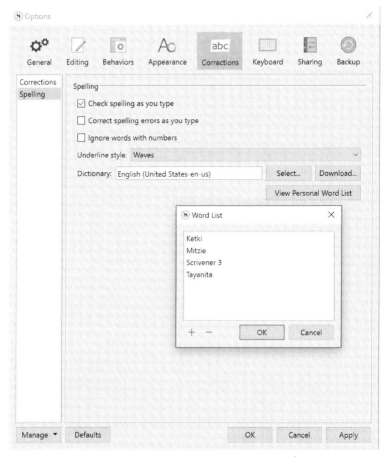

FIGURE 60: Editing Your Word List for the Spellchecker Tool

Incidentally, this is also where you can set preferences for automatic capitalization of sentences and the word I.

If you have long, complex names, you can also set up substitutions here. If you want Scrivener 3 for Windows to use curly quotes by default, this is where you set it up.

Name Generator

I don't know about you, but one of my biggest challenges in writing comes from the need to find names for my characters. When I first started writing, I couldn't imagine why this would be an issue. Now that I have written over thirty books, I understand the dilemma. Fortunately, Scrivener 3 has a tool to help with this problem.

If you choose Edit ▸ Writing Tools ▸ Name Generator, it will bring up a tool which allows you to search for names. You can set the complexity of the name you want and can even add custom name dictionaries. When I first discovered that I could add custom name dictionaries, I searched the web to find some. Finding none, I discovered I could create my own by going to baby naming sites and choosing my own. I have since learned that Literature and Latte's community board has several lists available to create custom name dictionaries.

You can generate the names by gender and have the name generator try to add alliteration to the first and last name, use initials or add a middle name.

To add a custom dictionary, click on the + in the name generating tool. There are several name dictionaries available from the Literature and Latte website. You can create your own from genealogy or baby naming sites. Save the list of names as a .CSV or .TXT file so you can import it.

Adding custom dictionaries to this tool makes it much more powerful. This is especially true if you are writing period-specific fiction.

Dictionary, Thesaurus and Other External Tools

You can easily link to a dictionary, thesaurus, Google and Wikipedia through Scrivener. Select a word or phrase in your manuscript and right-click. Choose writing tools from the menu and select one of the options. Opening these tools within Scrivener 3 is a particularly helpful option if you are trying to write distraction free. I don't know about the rest of you, but if I leave my work to go search for something on Google or Wikipedia, I get distracted and forget to get back to my writing. Accessing these tools through your Scrivener window cuts down on your chances of being distracted.

The dictionary Scrivener 3 uses is based on your system settings. If you need to change it for any reason, you can do so under File ▸ Options ▸ Corrections. You can also set up a bunch of other options from this menu to make it easier to type or dictate your document. I am a fan of the automatic capitalization of sentences. When I'm tired, I often forget to capitalize the first word in a sentence.

As an aside, one of my favorite language tools is a site called WordHippo.com. Unfortunately, I have not found a way to substitute this site for the existing thesaurus in Scrivener 3.

Substitutions, Transformations and Text Tidying Tools

The difference between a mediocre manuscript and one that looks polished can come down to the small details. Fortunately, Scrivener 3 has several tools to help you deal with the fussy minutia. These tools come in the form of substitutions, transformations and text tidying.

One of my favorite tools is the substitutions feature. This option on the edit menu allows you to substitute the type of quotes you use. I prefer to use curly quotes, but others do not. Scrivener gives you the option. You can also automatically format em dashes and ellipsis using substitutions.

There are many options under transformations. You can change the case of your text, convert your curly quotes to straight quotes and vice versa, and change the format of in-line annotations.

The tools under the text tidying menu are very helpful. You can delete tabs, multiple lines and spaces project-wide, among several other options.

One of the other places you can perform rudimentary text cleanup functions is in the Compile menu. You can click on the gear and remove hyperlinks, highlighting and leading spaces. There are other settings here too.

After my editor has finished working with my manuscript, I copy and paste each chapter back into Scrivener because I treat Scrivener files as master files. I find the Transformations tool under edit to be very handy. In Scrivener 3, they introduced a feature to remove small caps. It makes me want to do cartwheels because it makes it easy for me to remove small caps and have a clean, tidy manuscript.

Now that we've discussed how to create a manuscript and how to use tools to make it better, I'm going to talk about tools to search your manuscript.

CHAPTER 7

The Art of the Search

A side from the new compiling tool, the single most improved feature in Scrivener 3 is its enhanced abilities to search.

The quick search bar is one of my favorite new tools. In this section, we will discuss both the new quick search feature and the regular search feature—including project search and replace.

Quick Search

Unlike a standard project search, quick search brings up the first ten incidents of a word or phrase. This makes correcting errors during the editing process so much easier. For example, one of my proofreaders goes through my documents and finds the mistakes. When she identifies them for me, she lists a few of the surrounding words. With the new quick search feature, I can just plug those into the quick search bar and come up with the precise location of the error. Personally, I believe this one feature is enough to warrant an upgrade from Scrivener 1.

You can perform a quick search by going to Edit ▸ Find ▸ Quick Search or by pressing CRTL ⇧ G.

As I stated earlier, if you have entered progress targets into your project, the quick search bar will show both your overall progress and your daily progress. The immediate accessibility of this visual aid is a powerful motivator for me. The colors of the bar on top change depending upon how far you have progressed in your project. The default colors for this are red, yellow and green. Although you can, as I have, assign your own color scheme. This is done by choosing File ▸ Options ▸ Appearance ▸ Target Progress Bars ▸ Colors.

Although I love the new quick search tool, it has some limitations. For example:

Quick Search only shows the first ten search results in context. If you need to search more than the first ten, you must click on Full Project Search which brings you to the traditional search results.

Still, if you can search with a few words or a phrase, this feature is spectacularly helpful, even with its limitations.

Sometimes, the quick search tool is not robust enough and you will need to do a full project search using Project Search.

Project Search

Users of earlier versions of Scrivener will no doubt recognize Project Search. You can access this tool by clicking the magnifying glass on your toolbar or by clicking Edit ▸ Find ▸ Project Search The keyboard shortcut for this feature is CTRL G, CTRL S.

Although the Project Search function is powerful and can be customized to include specific files, documents or collections, it has limitations. Unlike Quick Search, the program does not lead you directly to the word you searched for. Instead, it simply highlights the search words in each folder or document. You can manually search for the highlighted words. If you have a long document, this can take a substantial amount of time.

Fortunately, Scrivener does have a way to make this process a little less painful using the Find feature (CTRL F). After you have clicked on the magnifying glass in the toolbar, it will bring up a list of the folders or documents in your binder which contain the words you have searched for. Place your cursor on the list, and press CTRL A to select the whole list. Then, press CTRL F to bring up the find box. If you choose next, Scrivener will toggle through and highlight each incident of the word in the search results. This approach is faster than manually searching for each search result.

You can place limits on what files Search in Project examines. You can search the whole project, documents within the project, or for specific formatting by clicking the arrow beside the magnifying glass in the tool bar.

If your search ever produces unexpected results, check to see if you have applied a search filter here.

Sometimes, a search may produce an overwhelming number of results. You can narrow your results by using words you want to exclude from your search. To use a negative search word, place a hyphen in front of the word you'd like to exclude.

You can also limit your search by create date or modify date. Simply right click on the magnifying glass and adjust the search parameters.

When I am writing fiction, I have a list of words I always remove before sending my work to beta readers or my editor. When I search for these words, I will frequently limit the scope of the search to a chapter or a small group of chapters, so I don't become overwhelmed by the editing task.

If you use Project Search and you have a difficult time seeing the highlighted words, remember, you can always change the color of the highlight in preferences.

Personally, I like to assign a neon color to the highlight so it's easy to locate in a long document.

Project Replace

Project Replace is a powerful tool. Because I use voice recognition software, I use this tool frequently to remove extra spaces placed in my documents by Dragon Professional Individual 15.3. However, it's also a great tool for changing a character's name midstream or when you are modifying a previous project for a new project.

Project Replace does exactly what it says. It searches your whole project for a particular word or character and replaces them with something else.

You can use Project Replace by going to Edit ▸ Find ▸ Project Replace or choose the icon on your toolbar.

Always double check your input into this tool because you cannot undo the changes made when you use this tool.

Trust me, making a mistake here can be catastrophic. One time, I was trying to replace two spaces with one space and somehow I got distracted and forgot to put the space in the replace box. Every place I had two spaces in my document now had no spaces. It took a long time to re-edit my document after my oversight.

The Project Replace tool is customizable, you can tell it to search and ignore capitalization and you can choose which items the function affects. For example, if you don't want the changes you made to affect your Snapshot or your Synopsis, you can simply uncheck those options. In fact, I recommend not including your Snapshot in Project Replace. Additionally, I recommend that you take a Snapshot before doing anything which can impact your entire document.

CHAPTER 8

An In-Depth Look at the Binder

s I've said several times, the Binder is the backbone of your project in Scrivener. It gives you an overview of your document and allows you to move information around without copying and pasting. The philosophy behind Scrivener is to allow authors to write however they feel comfortable. Aside from the mandatory files in Scrivener—the Draft Folder, the Research Folder and Trash—all other entries into your Binder are entirely up to your discretion.

If you are the type of author who likes to write all your thoughts at once with no structure, Scrivener can accommodate that. Conversely, if you prefer to divide your manuscript up into many scenes of varying degrees of detail, Scrivener can work with that too.

At the heart of this flexibility is the Binder. You are no longer confined to writing chronologically. Further, all of your information, manuscript and resources can be kept in one location. So, if you typically write your scenes in separate documents in

153

a word processor like Microsoft Word and then try to copy and paste them into a coherent document when you have finished your manuscript, you will find Scrivener much easier to work with. Scrivener 3 does this work for you.

In this chapter, I'll share some tips to make it easier to work with the Binder.

Working with Files

In Scrivener, your manuscript folders go into your Draft Folder. This folder may be named something different depending upon the template you started with. In some, it's called manuscript or screenplay. Whatever it's called in your project, your writing goes in the top folder in your Binder.

If you are using a Scrivener template, Scrivener places a help file in the top folder of each template. It summarizes the features of each individual template. I urge you to take a few moments to read it. These tip sheets give a lot of helpful information about special features in each individual template. These templates are often customized to meet specific needs with title pages, style guides, character and plot sheets as well as demonstration projects.

If you want to make adjustments to an already existing template, make a temporary project and then press the ALT key as you click Create. Then, make your changes and save the project as a template.

There are several ways to insert a new file or document into your Binder. You can click on the big green + in the toolbar, or, you can click on the folder with the + in the footer status bar, or you can add it under Project in the Menu, or you can right-click on an existing folder in your Binder and click on add. The keyboard shortcut CTRL ⇧N will also create a new folder.

When you add a folder to Scrivener, it will have new folder as the default name. You can change this by clicking in your synopsis or on the name of the file itself in the Binder.

For most purposes, it does not matter whether you add documents or folders in Scrivener 3. There are slight differences in the visibility of sub-folders in your editing window and the default scene separators. Other than that, they function remarkably the same.

Scrivener makes it easy to tell what type of content is in a file or document by its appearance. The mandatory folders have their own specific icons, and if you add new files or documents to your project, the appearance of these will vary.

If you enjoy working on sections of your manuscript out of order, it is simple to tell which files have content and sub-folders. In the graphic below, I have shown eight levels of folders. I could have continued to add more levels had I chosen to. This graphic is just to illustrate the different folder icons based on the content within them.

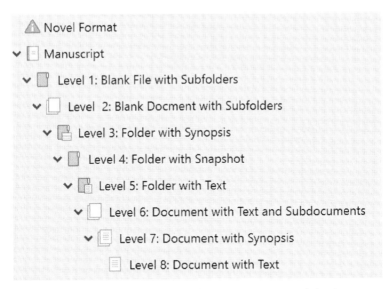

FIGURE 61: Types of Folders Within Scrivener 3 and the Icons Which Represent Them Based on Content

The different levels of files are not only aesthetically pleasing, as you navigate through your document, they come into play later on when you are assigning Section Types. You can elect to assign Section Types to your files or documents differently depending on the level in your Binder.

In my opinion, the easiest way to change the level of a file or document in your Binder is to use the Move buttons. These are arrow key icons which you can add to your toolbar. Alternatively, you can click and drag a folder or document to another location in your Binder or to a different level. There are several keyboard shortcuts which move the level of your folders or documents.

- Edit ▸ Move ▸ Move Down or CTRL↓
- Edit ▸ Move ▸ Move Left or CTRL←
- Edit ▸ Move ▸ Move Right or CTRL→
- Edit ▸ Move ▸ Move Up or CTRL↑

I move files quite a bit when I am editing. Sometimes, a chapter works better with the scenes in a different order.

To make it easier for you to differentiate your folders in a project, you can change the icon without changing the file type. To do this, right-click on the folder or document and choose Change Icon. If Scrivener 3's selection is not to your liking, you can add your own icon files through manage custom icons on the custom icon menu.

The ability to change the icon on each folder can be helpful. I use this feature when I want to mark where I have left off in my Binder. I right-click on the document in question and then change the icon to a star. The next time I open this project, I'll know exactly where I left off because the folder will now have a star beside the name instead of the file.

If you are anything like me, many of your manuscripts have common elements between them. This could be your copyright page, your backlist, or your author information. Additionally, you could have a story bible, plot sheets, character sheets or location sheets applicable to multiple documents.

One of my favorite ways to move folders between documents is to highlight them and drag them between projects.

To do this, make sure your projects are open in separate windows and minimize your window. Then, click on the Window menu and choose Bring All to Front. After you have done this, you can have two documents open in Scrivener at the same time. Select the files you want to move to the other file and then just click and drag those files to the Binder in the new project. You can move multiple files at once as long as they are selected in the Binder of your donor document.

 If you are moving files with the same name, make sure you move the old files to the trash first.

For example, if I am updating an old book list with new information, I need to throw away the old files which contain my book list before dragging the new ones in. Failure to do this can cause confusion. I know this from personal experience. Trust me, save yourself the hassle. You can always drag the old files out of the Trash Folder if you change your mind.

If you have a document or file within your Binder that has been set up the way you prefer to work, you can duplicate the folder and its sub-folders by using CTRL D. If you want to duplicate the folder without sub-folders, you can press CTRL⇧D.

 Don't forget, you can change the appearance of a folder in your Binder with your label colors.

I use this feature a lot because I write novels with dual points of view. It is easier for me to keep track of whose voice I'm writing in if I assign each character a specific label color. I frequently work with multiple projects at once. So, I try to make certain my character label colors are completely different.

The Power of the Right-Click

I know it seems silly to give a function like right-click its own section. However, I want to highlight this simple solution so you remember it exists. The right-click menus in Scrivener will help you navigate more efficiently. Each mode in the group mode has its own contextual menus which come up when you right-click.

If you right-click on any file in the Binder, a menu will pop up with several popular options for working with your manuscript. This is usually how I assign Section Types or change the status of my files.

Right-clicking after you've selected folders or documents in your binder allows you to copy those files to another project. Make sure you have the second project open when you try to use this tool.

The right-click function is context dependent. For example, it won't let you delete your Draft Folder and if you click on the Trash Folder, you will have the opportunity to empty your trash. (I don't recommend emptying your trash until you are completely finished with your project.)

Keep in mind that you can use the right-click function to add folders to your bookmarks. So, if you have details in one chapter you need to refer back to when writing another, you can just bookmark one file to the folder you are working with. This is also a good way to work with your story bible or character sheets if you have them in your Research Folder.

If you drag items from the binder of one project, into the bookmark tab of another project to share bookmarks, Scrivener will store a special external direct link to the individual items you dropped. Double-clicking this bookmark will load the original project if necessary and open the item you linked to within it.

If you like to navigate between documents in your project with links, you may find the Copy Document Link function helpful. It can be reached by right clicking anywhere on the Binder and navigating to the bottom of the menu which pops up.

Odds and Ends

We've talked extensively about using keyboard shortcuts or the tool bar icons with the blue arrows to move your files within the Binder. However, there is another way to move your folders up and down the Binder. You can click and drag them where you need them. A blue line will appear where Scrivener plans to put your folders or documents. You can pull it to the left and right to determine where it goes in the hierarchy.

If you write with multiple editors open, you might find the Binder Selection settings helpful. You can choose whether to have Scrivener navigate to the same place in both editor windows. Personally, I like the fact that in Scrivener if I make a selection in one view it automatically makes the same selection in the other editing window. For me, it helps ensure that I am working in the same document. However, other people may not like this feature so much. Fortunately, like most everything else, Scrivener 3 allows you to choose how to use its features.

This feature is located under the Navigate menu. Unless you have more than one editor window open, the Binder Selection choices will be grayed out. If you want Scrivener to select the same folder or file in both windows, you can click on the Both Windows Option. If you are editing and need to have your entire file structure available in the outline or Corkboard Mode, set this feature to change only the current editor.

 You can use Scrivener to automatically generate a table of contents. Although, be careful not to duplicate this in your Compile settings or you will have two.

If you are compiling to an e-book format, there will be an additional icon on the top left-hand side of the Compile Pane which allows you to set your preferences. If you don't want to add a table of contents here, you can uncheck the boxes in this menu.

 If you do not want your sub-folders to be in your manually generated table of contents, collapse them in your Binder before you create a table of contents document.

To create your own table of contents, add a new document or folder where you want the table of contents to be. Then, name the file Contents or Table of Contents. Next, choose the files or documents you want to be featured in the table of contents. Don't forget to include your front and back matter if you want them listed in the table of contents. After everything is high-lighted in your Binder, click on Edit ▸ Copy Special ▸ Copy as TOC. Go to the folder you created and paste the contents of your clipboard into your Scrivenings window. When this is done, you can format your table of contents any way you wish using Scrivener's formatting tools.

A manually entered table of contents is a static document. If you change the order of your chapters in your Binder, you need to find the table of contents you created and go through the steps again to update it.

Do you have an overwhelmingly long or complex binder? Many authors I know choose to use one project for an entire series. This can create a daunting binder. However, Scrivener 3 for Windows has included a tool to deal with this. It is called Hoist Binder. This function allows you to essentially zoom in on a folder within your binder. Simply click on the file in the binder you want to use and choose View ▸ Outline (the option below Zoom) ▸ Hoist Binder. After you've done this, all the folders in your binder are hidden except for the one you selected and its subfolders. When you want to go back to viewing your entire binder, choose View ▸ Outline (below Zoom) ▸ Unhoist Binder.

Another handy tool included in Scrivener 3 for Windows is the ability to highlight a particular folder or file in your Binder as a Binder Separator. So, for example, if you are working with a book with several parts, you can highlight the start of each part and designate it as a separator to make it easier to find in your Binder. To do this, highlight the folder you want to emphasize and right-click. Then, select Show as Binder Separator from the drop-down menu.

Quick Reference Windows are a great way to work with your reference materials or other important information because you can float these windows on top of your editing pane. To open a file as a Quick Reference Window click Navigate ▸ Open ▸ As Quick Reference.

If you would like to know how many subfolders are in each folder or document in your binder, you can choose to show that number. Go to View ▸ Outline (below Zoom) ▸ Show Subdocuments in Binder.

Are you a notetaker? If so, you may love the Scratchpad Panel within Scrivener 3 for Windows. The Scratchpad is a floating window that allows you to take notes while you are working in other applications (as long as Scrivener is running in the background). To access this, choose CTRL ↑ 0 or select Window ▸ Show Scratchpad. This is a toggle command, so use the same command to make the window disappear.

Now that we've discussed the Binder in greater detail, I'll move on to discussing Scrivenings.

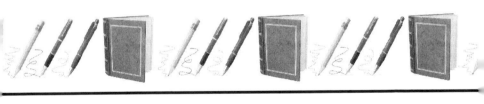

CHAPTER 9

Mastering Scrivenings

S crivenings is one editing mode within group modes. It is just a fancy way to refer to the portion of Scrivener which looks like a word processor.

In many ways, the Scrivenings section functions just like a traditional word processor.

Unlike traditional word processors, the way you view the Scrivenings pane doesn't need to have anything to do with how the final outlook appears.

For example, you may write in hot pink Comic Sans just for fun, but your output in the compiler can be a nice, sedate Times New Roman.

In the Scrivenings window, you can use the highlight tool and format the text different colors to show areas you need to edit or different character points of view.

When you Compile, you can choose not to show your font colors or highlights.

Remember, if you want to type or dictate in a distraction free environment, you can use the compose mode. If you turn on typewriter scrolling, the cursor will stay in the same spot as you continue to write or dictate.

If you want your document to appear as it might when it is compiled, you can set the styles to resemble your settings in the Format Compile Window and choose page view. Just make sure you set up the proper page size and margins under File ▸ Page Setup first.

Right-clicking while you are in Scrivenings, will bring up a contextual menu. One option on this menu is to split your document. If you select some existing text, it will become the name of the folder Scrivener 3 creates.

You can monitor your word count and progress toward any targets you have set in the Footer Status Bar in the Scrivenings mode.

If you need to get an accurate word count of the current section you are working on within a Scrivenings session, you can use the selection counting feature with the Edit ▸ Select ▸ Select Current Text command. Using this command will select only the text of the current section you are editing.

You can navigate between pages by clicking on the piece of paper or the arrows on either side in the footer status bar.

If the paper is checked beside your target, it means it has been selected to be included in your compile settings.

There are some features available in Scrivener 3 which I didn't discuss in-depth earlier. One of these involves using pictures in your Draft Folder.

Working with Images

I frequently insert pictures into my manuscript (particularly when I write nonfiction).

Scrivener 3 is structured in a way that prevents you from directly dragging a picture into your Draft Folder.

Typically, pictures are restricted to the Research Folder. However, if you use Insert Image from File (CTRL G, CTRL J), you can place an image file in your manuscript. You can also use a link to an external source.

Using a link to a file instead of an actual image may be helpful if you don't have the final image for your document.

The link just acts as a placeholder. However, for your final manuscript, you may want to insert the pictures into your manuscript, since you may not control access to the files on an external server.

Once you have added an image to Scrivener, you can click on it and resize it and adjust its resolution and the title of the picture. Unfortunately, in Scrivener you cannot wrap text around your image. If you want the image in your manuscript to include wrapped text, you'll need to compile your document to be edited in a different program like InDesign or Microsoft Word.

Be aware that adding images to your Scrivener file will increase your file size. Depending upon which royalty plan you use to list your books on Amazon, using images may significantly reduce the royalties owed to you.

Just as an aside, if you are writing a manuscript that includes screenshots, the resolution of your screenshots depends on your monitor. Set your monitor to the highest resolution possible.

In the Compiler, you can have Scrivener resize your images depending upon your output. This is very helpful when you are compiling to Microsoft Word. It saves you time in preparing your manuscript for printing.

If you plan to use images as your section breaks, they need to be placed in your Binder. These images go in the Research Section. Click and drag them from Windows Explorer. The rest of the work will be done during the compiling process. I will discuss using custom section breaks in Chapter 12.

Adding Math Equations

Sometimes, functions in Scrivener 3 need an outside program to be utilized. Such is the case with math equations.

You can insert math equations into Scrivener 3. However, you need an external program called Math Type. This is a subscription-based service that costs around fifty dollars a year. However, if you write textbooks or research papers that frequently feature math questions, it might be worth the expense.

Tables

You can use tables within Scrivener. To insert a table, you can right-click in the editor while in the Document Mode or click on Format ▸ Table ▸ Table.

The insert table function in Scrivener 3 for Windows works much the same way as tables in other word processing programs. (Although, there are fewer options for changing the appearance of the tables.) If you are working with a table, the right click menu becomes contextual in Scrivenings and will bring up several options related specifically to tables, including the option to remove the table and restore the text to normal.

 Keep in mind when using tables in e-books, every device displays e-books differently, and readers may have their own choice of font and line spacing. Therefore, your table may not appear as you expected. If you need your table to remain unchanged by the reader, you need to save your table as a picture.

However, make sure the picture is small enough to fit on one page. Most e-readers don't cope very well with pictures that need to span more than one page.

I work almost exclusively in the Scrivenings pane, however there are other views. Next, I will talk about working with the Corkboard Mode.

CHAPTER 10

Working with the Corkboard

I f you love sticky notes and index cards, the Corkboard Mode might be for you. It's like a virtual bulletin board, which allows you to manipulate your files without having to use copy and paste.

In this mode, you can easily write a synopsis for each section of your book or work with the synopsis automatically generated by auto fill. Additionally, you can move files around in the Corkboard Mode before committing them to your Binder by working in Free-form Mode.

In this section, I'll discuss this unique view and how to incorporate it into your workflow.

Manipulating Index Cards

The way you work with index cards has been upgraded and expanded in Scrivener 3 for Windows in some exciting ways.

You can still work with them the traditional way with each card presented in order from side to side or top to bottom. By choosing the top layer of any nested folders or documents in your Binder and switching to Corkboard Mode, you can see all the folders underneath the folder or document you selected. If you see a stack of index cards on your corkboard, that means another level of documents or files exists. To make these appear, just click on the icon on the index card. To further customize your index cards, you can add a status stamp by pressing F10, or you can show labels F9 or keywords ⇧F9.

A synopsis generated from the first few words of your document or file may appear on the index card. However, as soon as you type over that information with a new synopsis, it will appear in black. This synopsis will carry over to your outline and the Inspector in your Binder.

You can click on and drag the index cards to change the order in which they appear. However, unless you are in free-form mode, any changes you make in the order of your index cards will appear in your Binder.

If you want to try out an arrangement of your index cards without it affecting your Binder, you need to be in Free-form.

To enter Free-form mode click on the Free-form Option on your footer status bar. When you are in Free-form Mode, the word Commit will appear by the Free-form button. When you are ready to change your Binder, just click this button.

Scrivener 3 has added a new powerful view called Arrange by Label. (This is a toggle switch on your Footer Status Bar. It switches back and forth between the Arrange by Label view and traditional corkboard view.) You can have your cards follow a horizontal or vertical line. This is helpful when you assign labels for points of view, discrete periods of time, or to specific characters. By visually seeing your chapters follow a particular line, you can more easily determine if your chapters are balanced in terms of point of view or if each character has enough chapters for the role they play in your story. Below is an example of using Arrange by Label in a romance novel I wrote which contained several points of view.

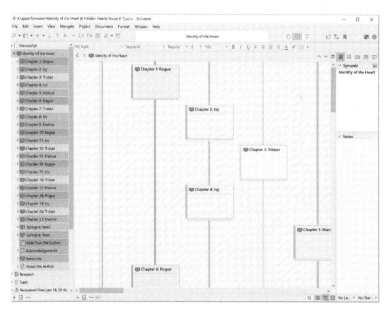

FIGURE 62: Arrange by Label in Scrivener 3

When using the Arrange by Label view, you can change the label on a particular card by dragging it to a different line. This will change the label and the Inspector, the Outline Mode and when you use the compiler.

As with files, you can press CTRL while you click on index cards to select multiple cards. Once you have selected multiple cards, you can move them around your corkboard or copy them to another project by right clicking on the Corkboard and choosing Copy to Project.

By changing Scrivener's behaviors to Allow Drop-ons in Corkboard under File ▸ Options ▸ Behaviors ▸ Dragging and Dropping, you can stack cards with other cards, just as you would drop items onto others in the Binder or Outliner.

In addition to moving index cards around on your Corkboard, you can change the appearance of the cards themselves.

Changing the Appearance of Your Corkboard

You can change the appearance of your index cards by clicking on File ▸ Options ▸ Appearance. Then, in the left panel select Corkboard. Personally, I find the font in the index cards a little difficult to see. Therefore, I always enlarge the font. You can also change the way your index card appears by adding lines or rounded corners.

You can adjust the appearance of the index cards by clicking on the four index cards in the lower right-hand corner of the

Footer Status Bar while you are in Corkboard Mode. This setting will allow you to change the number of cards that appear in a row and the size of the index cards. Additionally, you can check the box so that your cards scale up and down in proportion to the size of your Scrivener 3 window.

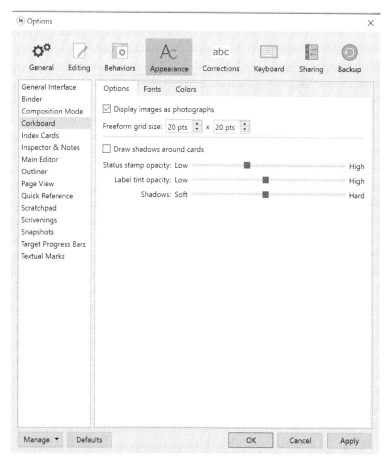

FIGURE 63: Changing the Appearance of the Corkboard in Options

Labels and Keywords

Labels and keywords really shine in the Corkboard Mode. You can now choose for your label colors to show on just the edge (F9) or on the whole card (F7). You can access this on the menu by clicking on View ▸ Use Label Colors in.

As I've mentioned before, labels are incredibly flexible. You can track point of view, plot lines, beats, locations and timelines by using labels or keywords. You can customize both the labels and the keywords to match your needs. Keywords will appear as little chips on the edge of your index card. Unlike labels, you can assign multiple keywords to a single chapter. With labels you can use only one.

I would be remiss if I didn't talk about assigning a status to your cards. The status settings are at the bottom of your inspector panel. For example, you can indicate that you are in the third round of revisions or that you've already checked a chapter with a grammar checker. If the status you wish to use it is not on the list, you can simply click on the edit button and add it.

By pressing F10, you can make your status appear across your cards

You can set the opacity of this stamp under Preferences (CTRL+). Status Stamps can give you an overview of your project in one simple glance.

The Corkboard and Index Cards are a handy way to look at your project. However, sometimes they don't contain enough information. For that, the Outline Mode is a good alternative. We will talk about the Outline Mode in the next chapter.

CHAPTER 11

Drilling Down the Outline

There are some modes in Scrivener I don't utilize as often as others, and I forget how helpful they are. The Outline Mode is one of those views for me. After all, I am a dyed-in-the wool pantser.

However, I occasionally like to work in the Outline Mode because it helps me get an overall picture of my whole document, lets me see if chapters are unbalanced, and discover plot holes. I like to show the number of words in each chapter and scene. That way, I can see if a scene is dragging on and may need to be divided. Conversely, I can also see if a particular chapter is exceptionally light on content. Additionally, I can see the flow of a document from start to finish.

In this chapter, I'm going to give you some tips on how to customize your outline and navigate through it. Finally, I'll discuss ways to print your outline.

Navigating in the Outline

As we talk about the Outline Mode, it is important to remember that you need to select a level in your Outline, which has sub-folders in order for the outlining feature to work.

Generally, when I work in the Outline, I work from the highest level in my Binder. This view allows me to see my entire document in outline form. Much like the Binder, if you don't want to see every sub-folder, you can collapse each level by clicking on the little arrow next to the title of your document or by using the following keyboard shortcuts:

View ▸ Outline ▸ Collapse All ALT [
View ▸ Outline ▸ Expand All ALT]
View ▸ Outline ▸ Collapse to Current Level ALT + -

Interestingly, the Outline Mode functions a little bit like a spreadsheet. You can sort each column A to Z or biggest to smallest and vice versa.

Sorting the columns in Outline Mode does not affect your Binder or manuscript.

You can add new files or documents to your Outline just like you would in your Binder or Corkboard Mode. The + adds a document and the + in the folder adds a new folder. As in the Binder, you can change the hierarchy of a document or folder in your outline by using the blue arrow keys you may have placed in your toolbar or CTRL with the arrow keys. This works to move your folders or documents up and down your outline.

Any changes made to status, keywords, or labels will be updated in the Binder, Corkboard and the Inspector.

Customizing Your Outline

You can customize your outline to include the columns you need to see. For example, you can look at labels, keywords, status, targets, and the date the document was created or modified.

Add custom columns by using the Metadata in your Inspector.

You can change your Metadata and add categories by clicking on the icon that looks like a price tag in your Inspector or by clicking on custom columns under the list of options for the outline while in Outline mode. To choose these columns, just click on the arrow next to the Inspector in your header status bar. Alternatively, you can choose View ▸ Outliner Options to bring up a checkbox menu to choose from.

Reorganizing the order in which Scrivener presents your columns is easy. You just click and drag the columns to your desired location. This function does not change your Binder.

Labels and Keywords

Labels and keywords can be helpful when you're working in the Outline Mode. They are also very flexible and may be used for a variety of things.

For example, if you are a fan of using beats such as *Romancing the Beat* by Gwen Hayes or *Save the Cat* by Blake Snyder, you can assign each type of beat a different color label or keyword and add those values to your outline.

If you use a label, the color of the label will go clear across the line in your outline. If you use a keyword instead, it will show up as a small color block in the keyword column.

You can only assign one label per document or folder. However, you can assign several keywords. For example, you could use keywords to track time, location, character interactions or point of view.

FIGURE 64: Print Settings in Scrivener 3 for Windows

Printing your Outline

It's not intuitive, but you can print your outline as it appears in Scrivener 3. First, in the outline pane, make sure you are on a level which allows you to see all the parts of the outline you would like to print. Then go to Print Setup under the File menu. Once you are in this menu, choose Outlines. This will give you a menu which will allow you to choose which information in your outline you would like to print. When you are done choosing, click OK to close the window.

Next, go to File ▸ Print Current Document (or CTRL P). This will bring up a typical print screen. From that, you can either print it out on a regular printer or save it as a PDF. You can even choose to print to your OneNote file.

This is a good method to print out your Outline if you just want a quick copy. It's not fancy, but it works.

Another option for printing your manuscript as an outline is to use the Compile feature and choose one of the many outline formats available. To work with this successfully, you may have to create more Section Types in your document and apply them appropriately to match the outline formats in Scrivener 3. The list of available Section Types is listed in the middle pane under the Section Layout Pane. If you need to add more sections to your project to work with an outline format, go to Project ▸ then Project Settings. After you have assigned the appropriate Section Types, choose the folders you want to include in your outline and press Compile.

Now that you've learned about the Binder, Scrivenings, the Corkboard and Outline Mode, we can now talk about ways to output your document with the Compiler.

CHAPTER 12

Demystifying Compile

W hen I told people, I was planning to write this book, many authors confessed to me that they only use Scrivener 3 as a word processing program and organizational tool because they find compiling too daunting.

It makes me sad when I hear something like that, because—although it takes time to learn—compile is one of the most powerful features in Scrivener 3. In my opinion, the compile feature is the one thing that sets Scrivener 3 apart from other applications in which you could write your story.

The Compile feature gives you control over the formatting and the method of output.

I know many people prefer the simplicity of a program like Vellum. However, because the makers of Vellum had to make their program easy to use under all circumstances, they had to eliminate some flexibility and options. I own Vellum, but I only use it to create large print books. I have formatted my own books for years using Scrivener. (Yes, even in Scrivener 1 for Windows.) You can make professional, unique looking documents with Scrivener. The number of ways you can compile your manuscript without making any changes to it is astonishing. Of all the ways to output a document and compile, I've only used about four. I routinely compile into Microsoft Word—where I do my finish formatting to remove things like widows and orphans and make tiny adjustments to spacing. I now use .EPUB files to upload my manuscript to Amazon instead of .MOBI files. I have also compiled to a PDF and have compiled obfuscated files for NaNoWriMo.

If you are writing for NaNoWriMo and want to keep the contents of your manuscript secret while you validate your word count, output it as a .txt file and pick NaNoWriMo Obfuscated as your format type. This will produce a scrambled manuscript with your word count represented.

The options available for compiling and formatting compelling documents in Scrivener 3 are vast and limited only by your imagination.

Output Method

Using the same manuscript to produce files in different formats is one of my favorite features in Scrivener. Without making direct changes to a manuscript, you can produce a paperback or an e-book and virtually everything in between.

Like many other things in Scrivener, the choices are dynamic. So, if you create a PDF, the formatting options which appear in the Format Pane will differ from the ones presented to create a text document.

Step one in the compiling process is to choose the output of your document. However, before you even get to the compiling stage, I recommend that you click on File ▸ Page Setup and choose your page size and margins.

After you have chosen all of your page attributes and set your margins, now you are ready to complete step one of the compile process and choose your output. To bring up the compile menu, you can choose it from your toolbar, find it under File ▸ Compile (or press CTRL⇧E).

Output options are roughly grouped together by file type. For example, all the output methods that produce an e-book are together.

Just a side note—I used to produce .MOBI files using the KindleGen tool from Amazon. This is now obsolete. Amazon now offers Kindle Create and Kindle Previewer. If you have KindleGen on your system currently, you need to delete it to avoid a software conflict.

After much experimentation, I've determined creating a .MOBI file is an unnecessary added step. An .EPUB file does not display any differently or increase your delivery charge.

If you still need .MOBI files, my favorite way to create them is to use an external program like BookFunnel. BookFunnel is a great tool for distributing ARC copies and giveaways. Direct2Digital also has great formatting tools (even if you elect not to publish through them.

Amazon now requires EPUB files. If you still need them, I recommend creating MOBI files with an external program or converter.

Some folks like to use a free program called Calibre to perform conversions. It is not my favorite program for making MOBI files. It can throw a bunch of errors. For this reason, I prefer to use a program like Book Funnel.

Compile Pane

The Compile Pane has a list of files on the left-hand side of the window when you choose compile. This is how you tell Scrivener which files you want to include in your final product. Although it's relatively straight-forward, there are some things you need to watch for.

FIGURE 65: Selecting Files to Include in Compile in Scrivener 3

In the example above, I have circled the highest level in my Binder. In this case, it happens to be Manuscript. Whenever possible, this should be the level you compile.

When you are in split screen mode, the active window always has a blue status bar at the top of the window.

See the little funnel icon next to the files you want to include? It is actually a filter which allows you to exclude documents.

Be careful not to inadvertently filter the files included in the compiler.

As with many cautionary tales in this book, this one was inspired by true life events. Somehow, I had accidentally applied a filter. I wasn't aware of this setting, and it took me forever to come up with a solution.

Now that you have the proper file identified and new filters attached, you can choose which files or documents you want included in your document.

You can check these all at once or press down the ALT while you click one of the check boxes. This will select all the documents. If you want just a few removed, you can press the CTRL key while you are clicking in a box you have selected to unselect it.

Using my novel as an example, I'll tell you some of my selections and why I make them. I often sell my books at in-person events where I inscribe them. Therefore, I like to have a blank page before my title page. When I am compiling into Microsoft Word, I add two extra blank pages at the beginning before my title page and one blank page after my dedication. I do not select the file which contains the name of my book.

I happen to use the same front material for my paperbacks and my e-books. So, in this example, the Add Front Matter says Paperback Novel. However, you definitely don't need to do it this way. You could add different front and back matter depending on the output and the final destination of your manuscript. For example, if you are posting e-books, you might want to have a separate back matter for the ones which contain Amazon links and create a separate front and back matter section for the e-books you post elsewhere, which don't have Amazon specific links.

There is a little lock beside the front and back matter sections in the compiler. If you click on the locks, the front and back matter you have selected will remain consistent every time you use that output method.

After you've chosen which files or documents you want to include in your output, it is a good idea to make sure your Section Types have been chosen correctly. If you find one that's wrong or unassigned, you can click on the down arrow and choose the proper type.

You might notice that there are icons across the top of the Compile Pane. Much like the Inspector, each one has an individual purpose.

The first one, which looks like a list, displays which documents or files you want to include in your output. It also allows you to assign front and back matter folders (which reside in your Research Folder in the Binder). Finally, you can assign Section Types from this window.

The next icon represents Metadata. This is where you put your title and author information. Depending upon how you set up Scrivener, this may or may not be pre-populated.

 Always check your Metadata settings—even if you think you've Included the correct information.

I once published a book with the wrong title on every other page. I used a template created from another project and forgot to change the Metadata. Don't make my mistake—It's more than a little embarrassing.

You also have the option to add subjects and keywords here. Personally, I don't recommend it since your marketing strategies may change over time and it's easy to forget about this setting.

The next icon is the gear. Clicking on this will allow you to change many settings from whether you include the text color, highlighting, in-line annotations and footnotes, among others. These options will change depending on the output method you have chosen. One of the handiest settings here is the option to remove white trailing spaces.

I adjust my settings in this window depending on which output I am using. For example, if I am compiling books to use as paperbacks, I remove all the hyperlinks.

FIGURE 66: Optional Settings Under Compile in Scrivener 3

The next icon represents replacements. This feature will allow you to identify things you want replaced in your output. For example, if you have written a document for NaNoWriMo and avoided using contractions to increase your word count, you can set Scrivener to replace did not with didn't or you are with you're.

The replacement function is helpful when you are working with words with accent marks.

So, you can type the word in your document without accent marks but use the replace feature to substitute a more complex version using the proper accents.

The next icon only appears when you're working with e-books. It looks like a picture because it is where you add your cover photo.

If you want to use a cover on your e-book file, you need to drag your cover into the research section of the Binder.

For consistency, I always place mine right above my front matter folder.

The final icon may or may not appear depending upon your output selection. This icon allows you to set parameters for your table of contents in an e-book. You can choose what the section is called and how it appears. If you have already added a table of contents manually (as described in Chapter 8), unselect the boxes in this menu.

After you have chosen all of your folders or documents, set section layouts and adjusted your advanced settings, it is now time for you to move to the Format Pane.

Format Pane

As I described before, if the output method is equivalent to telling the print setter what you would like to create and the Compile Pane is telling the printer what you would like included in the final product, the Format Pane is equivalent to telling the printer what you would like your work to look like.

The Formats offered to you depend on the output method you choose. For example, there will be several more options for a .PDF document than there are for a simple text document.

Scrivener comes pre-populated with Formats to match your output. However, if none of those work for your project, you can adapt the existing Formats to suit your preferences.

You also have the option to create a Format from scratch. Personally, I find it easier to adapt an existing Format which is close, but not perfect for my project.

You can preview what each Format will look like when applied to Section Types in the Section Layout Pane. If you like how it appears, perfect! You are ready to move on to the next step. However, if you want to change things like spacing or font choice, you'll have to edit an existing Format or create your own from scratch.

To edit an existing Format, right click on the Format's name. Then choose Edit or Duplicate and Edit.

When modifying Formats, I strongly recommend you choose Duplicate and Edit, rather than changing the original Format.

When you click on this, you will be asked to save the Format under a new name. At this point, you have two options. You can save the Format under My Formats and it will be saved globally. Every project you create in Scrivener 3 will have the option to use this format. Conversely, you can save it under Project Formats and it will be available to that specific project.

The benefit to saving a format as a Project Format is that it attaches to your Scrivener file and other people who open your file will have access to the Format.

Adjusting Trim Size

Scrivener has many standard trim sizes available as menu choices. However, if you need to set up a different trim size, it is easy enough to do—although the menu options are somewhat buried. To access them, you need to be in the compile window. After you have clicked compile, right-click on the format you want to work with. This is a contextual menu. So, for example, if you are compiling an EPUB, the page settings won't be present. Make sure it says .doc, .RTF, or .PDF. If you've selected the proper output type, page settings will appear on the left-hand side of the window.

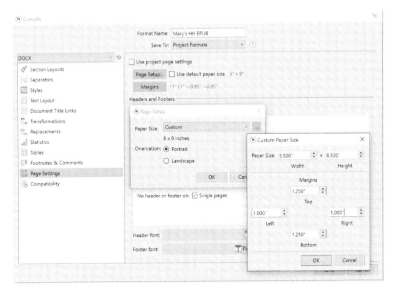

FIGURE 67: Adding a Custom Paper Size

If you want to change the trim size of your document, this is where you make those changes. Right click on the format you want to modify. If the format you want to use is not provided in the many options in the pre-populated drop-down list under Page Settings, you can add one of your own. Make sure the default paper size is not checked and then click on page settings. At the bottom of the list is an option called custom. If you click on the ellipsis, another menu will appear which will allow you to insert the measurements of your desired paper size. Additionally, you can set your margins here. Unlike the Mac version, you cannot give your custom size a specific name. However, when you save your format, the margins and page size should be saved. So, if you need to use the same format with different trim sizes, you can just make additional formats. I recommend you include the trim size if you have several.

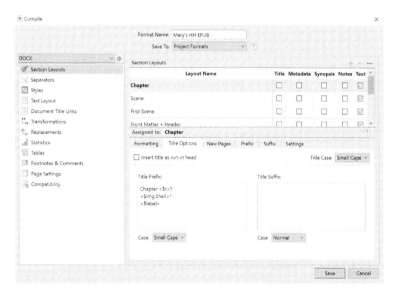

FIGURE 68: Modifying an Existing Format Within Scrivener 3

Users of earlier versions of Scrivener will recognize parts of this window. This is where you work with the nuts and bolts of how a format is created.

Scrivener uses placeholders to make formatting changes. In the above example, I am using a placeholder to number my chapters to look like Chapter One. Because I have selected small caps, it looks more like CHAPTER ONE. Then, I have an image I use across my series. Lastly, because I alternate my character's point of view, I use labels to identify them and the label appears in the chapter heading.

The output of the placeholders used in the example above looks like this:

CHAPTER ONE

JADE

"BARBARA ANN, WHY ARE YOU being such a drama queen about this? I thought we were getting matching Celtic friendship knots because I'm your best friend. Why did you let her choose the design first?"

The blonde sitting in my chair flips her hair back violently, almost screwing up my line. "Maybe you didn't get the first shot because you can't remember what to call me. The only person who still calls me Barbara Ann is my grandma — even *she* can remember to call me Lennox most of the time."

The girl who was whining looks really confused for a moment as she remarks, "Barbara — I mean Lennox — that doesn't make sense. It's not like we don't know your real name. We've been best friends since kindergarten. I don't get what's wrong with your name, but whatever."

The blonde in my chair huffs. "Ashley Nicole gets it. It bugs me that you don't. Maybe you aren't such a good friend, Allie."

FIGURE 69: EPUB Output Using Placeholders in Scrivener 3

Although you don't have to, you can use placeholders in various parts of your document. In part, they are used to number things or identify things within your manuscript. Here are some of the more common placeholders to identify your chapters and sections.

<$n>	Inserts numbers like 1, 2, 3
<$sn>	Inserts numbers like 1, 2, 3 in sub documents.
<$w>	Inserts lowercase word for a number like one, two, three.
<$W>	Inserts an uppercase word for the number like ONE, TWO, THREE.
<$t>	Inserts a title case word for number like One, Two, Three.
<$r>	Inserts lowercase Roman numbers i, ii, iii
<$R>	Inserts uppercase Roman numerals I, II, III
<$l>	Inserts lowercase letters for a number like a, b, c
<$L>	Inserts lowercase letters for number like A, B, C

These placeholders can be used to label chapters or in section headings or to label page numbers.

You'll note in several of my examples, I have an image placeholder. To use this, make sure the name of the graphics file in the research section of your Binder is the same as what you put in the placeholder. I use the same template for all of my fiction series regardless of the series. Each series has a different chapter heading graphic. So, after I drag my preferred image into the research section of the binder, I simply rename it Shell. There's nothing magical about this name, it just happens to be the name of the file I used the first time I set this format up. It is easier for me to change the name of the graphic in my binder than it is to adjust the placeholders.

There are many more placeholders available, for a list of them, consult the List of All Placeholders, located in the help section. This guide is quite comprehensive. Don't be overwhelmed. It is likely you'll only need a few of these placeholders.

To have Chapter 1 appear in your manuscript, you would place Chapter <$n> under title options.

If you want to adjust the spacing and font size in the title you just created, go back to the formatting tab. You can change the font, font size, font color and line spacing. Title prefixes and suffixes can be formatted in different ways.

To add to the confusion, there are actually two tabs that say prefix and suffix. This is to add additional information. If you want to include a location or date, you could use these tabs. So, if your novel includes two locations, you could create a style type for each.

By clicking on New Page, you can set your options for headings at the top of your page and whether you will be using small caps at the beginning of each chapter. If you have a blank line before the first line of text in your section, the small caps formatting will not show up.

The last tab is Settings. You can adjust how your indenting is handled based on the content of your document here.

You will have to set up each section layout separately. However, if you want to duplicate an existing section layout, click on the + after you have selected the section you would like to duplicate. Scrivener will place a new Section Type under the Section Layout you have selected. All the formatting will be carried over to the new section layout you have created. You can go in and make your changes to make it different from the one you just copied.

 Remember, if you create a new Section Layout here, you need to go to Project Settings to add the section type so you can assign it to your files or documents. Make sure you save your changes.

You can preview what your format will look like under the Section Layout Pane in the middle of the compiler page.

Now that you've applied your favorite format or created your own to apply to the files or documents you selected in the Compile Pane, now it's time to make sure Scrivener knows how to use those two types of information together. This is done in Section Layout Pane.

A Word about Separators

I would be remiss if I didn't touch on Separators. To access this menu go to Compile (CTRL ⇧ E) and then right click on the format you want to use. The separators menu is on the left-hand pane. Notice on the example below, PDF is chosen. If you choose another type of output, different options will appear.

201

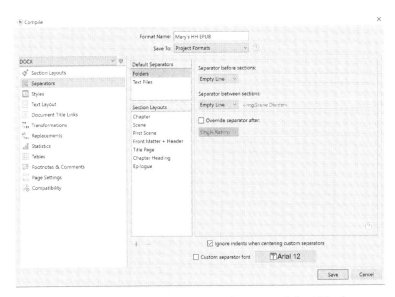

FIGURE 70: Setting Up Separators in Scrivener 3 for Windows

Okay, it's time to own up to another one of my mistakes. Normally, I don't think much about separators in Scrivener. I have special Section Types set up for my first scene and the rest of my scenes with special formatting. I put an image on the top of the scene section type and usually everything works just fine.

Until it doesn't.

This is one of those situations where I need to give a huge shout out to Bobby Treat for helping me understand why odd things were showing up in my table of contents.

I was taking a screenshot of a file I created using the new format I created for the relaunch of my series. I noticed the table of contents was terribly wonky. My sub-folders (which I name to make navigating around the quick search feature easier) were showing up in my table of contents. This was not what I wanted at all.

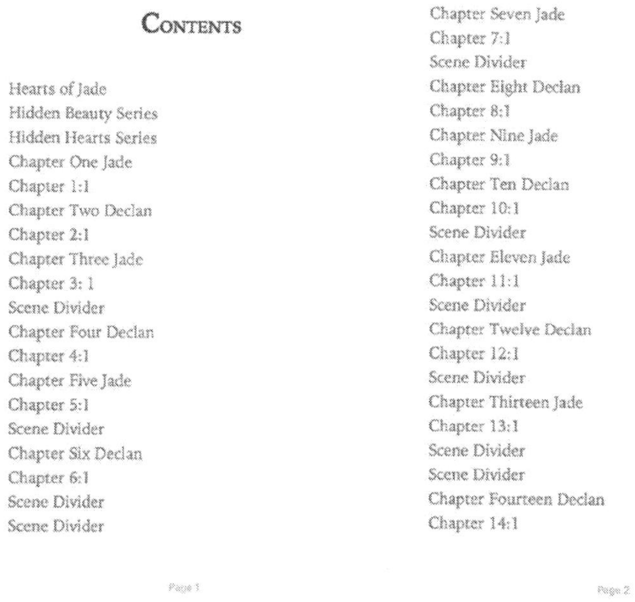

CONTENTS

Page 1

Page 2

FIGURE 71: Separators Incorrectly Applied in Scrivener 3

I was very confused because when I created this new series format, I meticulously copied and pasted everything from an existing format which was working just fine. I double and triple checked to make sure everything was as it should be. The formats appeared to be identical. But, they weren't operating the same because I forgot to change some settings in Separators.

I learned the hard way that folders and documents are not treated exactly the same in Scrivener as I had always understood. The default separators are different. I like to work in folders. I don't know why. I guess maybe a folder looks more impressive than a piece of paper in my Binder—I'm weird that way.

Anyway, long story short (okay, short-ish), because I was using folders for my scenes and I had not changed the Separator settings, it was triggering an entry in the table of contents.

By default, folders have a page break set up as its default separator. This works okay if you're working with chapters. However, I was working with scenes within my chapters.

On the other hand, documents in Scrivener have an empty line as the default setting, which does not trigger an entry into the table of contents or force a new page. Because of the way my manuscript is constructed, I needed to use a single return in my first scene and scene section layouts.

I left the page break as the default setting in my chapter, epilogue and front matter folders because I wanted a page break included. I also wanted these documents in my table of contents.

If you want, you can also choose a wingdings or webding to use in these blank spaces. There are already some default formats in Scrivener which use little graphics like this. If you want an example, the modern format uses them.

You need to set your separator preferences for each section type in your document.

Section Layout

The Section Layout Pane in the compiler is a new feature in Scrivener 3. Many people find this confusing. It doesn't have to be. Using my analogy of taking your manuscript to the print setter, you have now told the printer which documents you want in your book on the Compile Pane and identified which typeface, spacing and special formatting you want to apply in the Format Pane. Now, it's time to move on to the Section Layout Pane where you tell the printer which formatting you want to apply to each part of your manuscript.

When you first choose a format for your document, if you have never used it with that particular project, you will encounter a window with a big yellow warning. This warning is to inform you that you need to assign section layouts. There is a button for Assign Section Layouts.

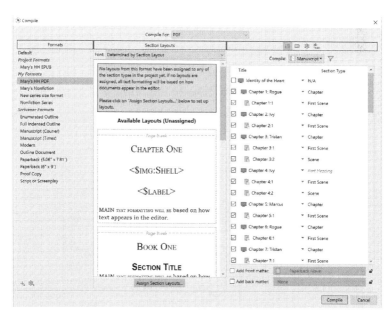

FIGURE 72: Assigning Section Layouts in Scrivener 3

When you click on this button, you will be presented with the Section Types you have used in your document. (If you wish to see more, you can click on a button to display the rest of your Section Types.) Next to that list, you will be shown the available Section Types for the format you have chosen. Now, it's a matter of matching them up.

You can either accomplish this by right clicking on a Section Type and choosing the Section Layout that corresponds with it from the drop-down list, or you can click on an individual Section Type and then click on the Format you want to use with it.

Final Steps of Compile

After you have accomplished this, you are ready to compile. The first thing that will happen when you click Compile is that you will be asked to save your document somewhere. This is a matter of choice, but I have a folder for each title I'm working on and a folder for draft manuscripts.

At the bottom of the window, you'll have the opportunity to have Scrivener open an application to allow you to check the quality of the work. This is an optional step, but I always use it to make sure everything is as I intended it to be.

You can overwrite files with new files with the same name. However, I don't recommend this. Just choose an entirely different name. This will help avoid confusion when you upload your file for publication. I always date my files and if I'm working with multiple files during the day, I also add military time.

Congratulations! You've successfully created a document in Scrivener. Hopefully, it's everything you dreamed. But, sometimes it's not and working with outside programs might be helpful. I'm going to discuss some of those next.

CHAPTER 13

Incorporating Scrivener into Your Workflow

Scrivener is a very powerful writing tool. It is comprehensive in nature. However, even Literature and Latte admits that the program is not designed to produce pristine finished work. Sometimes, it is helpful to use other programs in your workflow. This discussion will talk about some common options and how to efficiently work with outside people like beta readers and editors.

Personally, I use Scrivener 3 for almost everything. However, there are parts of the process of writing a book where I employ other programs such as Dragon Professional Individual 15.3, ProWritingAid, Photoshop and Microsoft Word. Sometimes, it takes a village to create a professional-looking manuscript. If you use other software resources while using Scrivener, it doesn't mean that you are a failure at Scrivener. The great thing about this program is that it enables you to use the parts you feel comfortable with but doesn't require you to know and use every function.

Working with External Programs

I frequently tell people I use Scrivener to write and format all of my books. This is true ... and false.

While I create, organize, write and format my books using Scrivener, Scrivener is not the only program I use. Because of the nature of my disability, I use Dragon Professional Individual 15.3. Without voice recognition software, I could not write. It's as simple as that.

Dragon is critical for my success, but it is not the only program I use to complete my manuscripts. I also perform my finish formatting in Microsoft Word, make chapter headings and title pages in Adobe Photoshop, and edit my work with ProWritingAid.

I don't work with Google Docs or Pages much, but I know other people do, so I will cover those.

Scrivener and Dragon

Unfortunately for me, Dragon Professional Individual 15.3 doesn't integrate as well with Scrivener 3 for Windows as Dragon Professional Individual 6.0.8 does with Scrivener 3 for Mac. For those of you who are not users of voice recognition software, some of this discussion may not make much sense. But I'll try to give you an overview.

Dragon Professional Individual 15.3 is a speech-to-text program offered by Nuance. Even though the Windows operating system offers speech-to-text abilities, they are not nearly as powerful as Dragon Professional Individual 15.3 for Windows.

Sadly, Dragon Professional Individual 15.3 does not have full text capabilities in Scrivener 3 for Windows. Translated, that means that although you can do straight dictation in Scrivener 3 for Windows using Dragon, it is not possible to correct your mistakes with the program. This is detrimental because Dragon Professional Individual 15.3 becomes more accurate as you correct any mistakes it makes.

There are two ways to work with Dragon and Scrivener 3. You can dictate directly or transcribe your files and import them into Scrivener. Each approach has its pros and cons, so I will discuss each briefly.

Direct Dictation

As I mentioned, dictating directly into Scrivener 3 for Windows is a little frustrating since I can't make corrections. Therefore, when I work on the Windows side of things, I use an application called Speech Productivity Pro.

Technically, Dragon has a program called DragonPad built-in to cope with programs which are not fully supported.

 DragonPad is prone to crashing. I don't recommend it.

If you are dictating into DragonPad, when it crashes, you lose all of your work. Speech Productivity (an add-on program available for nominal cost) fixes this weakness. In short, Speech Productivity Pro is everything DragonPad should be but isn't. It allows you to automatically save your dictation and dictate into a variety of high definition boxes with varying degrees of size and transparency.

If you don't want to use an add-on program, you can use OneNote, WordPad or text edit. Grammarly (the grammar checking program) also works as a great environment to receive dictation. Before I discovered Speech Productivity Pro, this was my preferred workaround for working in Scrivener.

To dictate fiction efficiently, I add my custom vocabulary words into Dragon, so I have to make fewer corrections.

Dragon has an odd glitch that could impact your work in Scrivener. It inserts extra spaces. To deal with this pesky issue, use project replace and type in two spaces in the Replace blank, and one space in the With blank. That should remove any extra spaces or, you can use the text tidying tool which has a setting to remove extra spaces. One place where Dragon can add extra spaces is at the beginning of the paragraph. To delete those, highlight the paragraph mark and copy it. Then, paste it into the Replace blank in Project Replace and add a space after it. In the With blank, just put a plain paragraph mark. This will delete the space before paragraphs everywhere except for the very first paragraph in your folder or document. That one you will have to delete by hand.

Another option is Dragon Anywhere. This is a subscription service from Nuance for a program which runs on both iOS and Android devices. It is not as full-featured as the desktop version of Dragon. However, many people find it helpful for dictating on the move. Dragon Anywhere requires Wi-Fi access.

I have used voice recognition software for thirty years. So, I am used to having the words appear in front of me on the screen. Therefore, I don't use transcription as much as I probably should. Many authors, including me, find that using transcription speeds up their dictation because they are not focused on correcting mistakes.

Transcription

Transcription is a great option for people who want to dictate away from their computer.

 Don't dictate while you drive.

I just have to put that out there. I know there are people who dictate while driving. However, as a former Disability Advocate, I have seen too many of my friends' lives destroyed by people who were driving distracted. I know we are all on deadlines, but please don't take the risk.

Even if you can't dictate while you're driving, there are many other places you can dictate for transcription. Many people do it while they take their dogs for a walk, wait for their kids to arrive in the pickup line at school, or even while they wait for an appointment.

Basically, transcription involves recording your voice and creating an audio file to upload to your computer so that a program like Dragon can turn it into text. Aside from Dragon, you'll need a recording device and a microphone.

You can either buy a small digital recorder with a USB card or, you can use your cell phone. Although I own two digital recorders, I prefer to use my cell phone.

Voice Record Pro is a program which records your speech and sends it directly to Dropbox, OneDrive, your email address, or several other places. This feature makes it convenient to use with the transcription setting in Dragon.

When you transcribe files, you can save them as .RTF files or Microsoft Word documents. If you use Microsoft Word documents, I suggest you import them into your Scrivener projects using Import and Split.

If you want more information on Dragon or transcription, the first two books of the Empowering Productivity series are about voice recognition software and integrating it into your writing process.

Now that I've talked about getting my words on paper, now I'll talk about my favorite tool for editing, ProWritingAid.

Scrivener and ProWritingAid

I can't say enough positive things about ProWritingAid. I have a lifetime subscription to this grammar checking tool. I believe it has made me a stronger writer. One of my favorite things about this tool is that it works directly with your Scrivener file.

 If you want to open your project in ProWritingAid, make sure you have closed your Scrivener project first.

If you've failed to do so, ProWritingAid will give you a warning message. It is not a good idea to work with multiple copies of your project. It can get confusing quickly and put your words at risk. If you haven't used ProWritingAid in a while and were frustrated by ProWritingAid's tendency to recognize Scrivener's coding as mistakes, recent upgrades have taken care of that little glitch.

I'm a very consistent writer. I repeatedly make the same mistakes. While I am still in Scrivener, I eliminate words I commonly overuse. These include that, just, pretty, so, little bit, and going to. I review one chapter at a time and limit my search parameters to one or two chapters, so the process doesn't become overwhelming. Doing this preemptive work saves me time in ProWritingAid. You may also want to remove any double spaces and make sure your quotation marks are consistent. ProWritingAid will mark them if one half of your quote has straight quotes and the other half is curly.

When you start ProWritingAid, you can run a variety of checks on your document. I use the combo report and fix a bunch of things at once. Consequently, I run the checks on one chapter at a time.

 ProWritingAid can get bogged down if you do a grammar check on a large document all at once.

While open in ProWritingAid, your project will look different. That's okay. Don't panic, your formatting will still be there when you reopen your project in Scrivener.

After you've made your changes, make sure you save them. If the save option is grayed out, you need to make one more change in your document. It's kind of a glitch in ProWritingAid. Usually, I can find a comma or yet another instance of a crutch word to delete. After I've made that last correction, ProWritingAid allows me to save.

Close ProWritingAid before you try to open your document back up in Scrivener. All your changes will appear in your Scrivener project.

Again, if you are working with Dropbox, make sure your project is completely saved. Scrivener files can be large. It could take some time.

I've told you how I get words on the paper and how I make them the best they can be, now I'm going to describe how I incorporate Microsoft Word into my publishing process.

Scrivener and Microsoft Word

Let me start this section by acknowledging that it is entirely possible to produce a PDF using Scrivener alone. For the most part, things turn out just fine. However, I have had issues with mirrored margins and orphaned text. This is one reason I do my finish formatting with Microsoft Word. I adjust the margins by putting in a gutter and adjust any spacing abnormalities by hand.

The other reason I use Microsoft Word is because virtually every editor I have ever worked with prefers to use it over Scrivener. Since I write with my pages mostly formatted, I just finish the job up in Microsoft Word before I give my manuscript to my beta readers and editors.

This is where Scrivener really shines. Sometimes, my readers and my editor get my work a couple chapters at a time. Using compile, I can compile only the chapters I need to give them.

I give my beta readers and my editor Word documents to allow them to use track changes. Even though Scrivener has a helpful revisions mode, it still doesn't make the changes for you. In this area, Microsoft Word has Scrivener beat by a mile, in my opinion.

I treat my Scrivener project as my master manuscript. Therefore, after I have made my edits and the readers have given their feedback, I move my work from Microsoft Word back into Scrivener. Personally, I do it one chapter at a time. It just gives me one more chance to look at my words against a different background than I used in Microsoft Word. Sometimes, I find typos during this process.

However, if you don't want to copy and paste your chapters one at a time, you can use Import and Split just like you may have done when you started working with your document.

Although some people have many copies of the manuscript in their Draft Folder, I recommend moving the old file to the Research Folder before performing the Import and Split function on your edited document.

The cleanup editing in Microsoft Word generally produces a beautiful document. However, I have an artistic streak a mile wide. So, I always have to dress it up a little. To do this, I use Adobe Photoshop. I also use Adobe Pro DC to produce my final PDF to upload to Amazon and Ingram Spark.

Scrivener and Adobe Photoshop

I've been known to make elaborate chapter headings for each character in my novels in addition to a title page. Even though I print my books in black and white, I still do my embellishments in color because more and more people are reading e-books on their cell phones and tablets which can display color files. These days, I don't create different chapter headings for each book because I want my series to look unified. However, I still use Photoshop to create my title pages.

HIDDEN BEAUTY BOOK 13

FIGURE 73: Title Page Created in Adobe Photoshop and Inserted into Scrivener 3

This is one I created for my upcoming work-in-progress. It's pretty, but large files can increase your delivery cost. So, when I save my title pages, I use the Export function in Adobe Photoshop and tell it to Save for Legacy. This setting allows you to preserve the appearance while still shrinking the file size.

Then, to use it in Scrivener, I make a folder in my front matter and name it the same as the title of my book. After that, I click on Insert ▸ Image From File.

If you are planning to make a paperback, make sure your title page is three hundred dpi or better.

The other Adobe program I use is Adobe DC Pro. This allows me to export a proper .PDF compatible with Ingram Spark. First, I use the export .PDF function in Microsoft Word to create my .PDF. It is important that you set the proper page size and margins within Microsoft Word before you do this.

Then, after I have created the .PDF, I open it in Adobe DC Pro and run a preflight check on it. Preflight is located under the Edit menu. Ingram Spark prefers to use PDF/X — 1a files. Running your PDF through this one last step helps make sure there are no issues while you upload to Ingram Spark.

Although I don't routinely work with Google Docs or Pages, many people do, so I'm going to talk a little about working in those two programs with Scrivener.

Scrivener and Google Docs or Pages

Although I don't know very many people who write directly into Pages, it has some beautiful formatting options and if you upload your manuscript to Apple, Pages has a mechanism to do that directly.

Scrivener cannot import documents created in Pages directly. Therefore, you'll need to export it to another format first. You can export to .RTF or a Microsoft Word document. Pages does a superb job of converting to Word documents.

Once you have created a Word document, you can use Import and Split to put it into folders in your Binder.

Interestingly, you can open Word documents in Pages and then save them as a Page document. So, if you want to take advantage of Apple's streamlined publishing process using Pages, you could compile a document from Scrivener into Microsoft Word and then convert that into a Pages document.

Google Docs is a favorite among authors, especially those who like to work collaboratively. I can see why. Your files are available anywhere you have Internet access and multiple people can collaborate on them without risking any data.

Google Docs has a voice typing tool with some odd limitations. It is missing basic punctuation like quotation marks, colons and semicolons. If your characters tend to cuss, Google Docs Voice Typing may not be the tool for you. Cuss words are censored in Google Docs.

 Like Pages, Google Docs can work with Microsoft Word documents and output them as well.

To work with a document you created in Google Docs in Scrivener, you'll need to export it as a Microsoft Word document. To do so, save the file to your Google drive. Click on file then download. There will be another menu available. You can save your document as an .RTF, a text file or a Microsoft Word file. As before, you can use Import or Import and Split to bring the Microsoft Word document into Scrivener.

Unfortunately, there is no standard software for writing that everyone uses. However, most people who haven't discovered Scrivener yet use Microsoft Word. This includes your beta readers and editors. So, next I'm going to talk about how to incorporate working with other people who use other software into your writing process.

Working with your Editor and Beta Readers.

Almost every beta reader and editor I've ever used prefers to work in Microsoft Word. I don't mind this because Microsoft Word has track changes which works far better than Scrivener's revision mode.

I try to vet beta readers carefully and I have a strong team now. However, every once in a while, I will get a new beta reader I haven't worked with before. In that case, I don't provide them with a Microsoft Word document. Instead, I issue a special .EPUB for them which I upload to BookFunnel. If they give me valuable feedback and want to continue being my beta reader, I move them up into my primary beta reading team. Those people get Microsoft Word documents directly from me.

Recent changes in Amazon's process means you don't actually have to upload a file when you post a preorder.

This policy change has made the process much easier for me. Now, once I have shared my book with my beta readers and editor, I don't put it back into Scrivener until after I have completed all the edits. (I used to do it after each round of feedback to make sure I had the most up-to-date manuscript available on Amazon for the preorder process.)

I work with the Microsoft Word document using track changes and, after I have completed all the edits, I copy and paste my Word document back into Scrivener one chapter at a time. It is entirely possible to use Import and Split for this function. However, I choose not to because pasting my document back in one chunk at a time allows me to take a last-minute look to find typos and continuity errors.

I use the Remove Small Caps feature under Edit ▸ Transformations to remove the small caps that I have imported from my Word document. Sometimes, you may have to reformat a paragraph that contains small caps and doing so can change the way they look. So, when it's back in my Scrivener file, I remove them to avoid this problem.

I always give my beta readers a final version of the book they've been working on to thank them for all their hard work.

If you are working with an editor or beta reader who gives you lots of comments, make sure you have deleted them all before you import your document back into Scrivener. I have seen them cause real havoc. It's easier to eliminate them in Microsoft Word.

When you are transferring your file back to Scrivener, use a slightly different text color in your editing window. That way, you will know which sections of your document you have already completed.

My process may not work for you; you need to adjust your workflow to whatever makes you comfortable.

Making the Process Work for You

I hang out on a lot of boards dedicated to the craft of writing and the subject of technology and how to properly use it comes up often. I'm always amazed when I read about everyone else's process because it's often different from mine. In this book, I have done my best to highlight things that worked well for me and caution you against the things that have not.

However, that doesn't mean you have to adopt my approach to using Scrivener.

One of the great things about this program is that you can adapt it to the way you work.

Some people only use Scrivener for the organizational features and write their documents in Microsoft Word. If that's what floats your boat, more power to you.

The goal is to make you as productive as you want to be. Scrivener can help with that, but don't feel like everyone's process has to be the same. My advice is to develop a workflow that works for you and adjust it as you learn new skills and grow as an author.

Next, I'm going to address some troubleshooting techniques for some common issues including how to restore your project from your backup, common compiling issues and how to work with Scrivener iOS with Scrivener 3 for Windows.

CHAPTER 14

Troubleshooting

Restoring from Backup

S ometimes, despite our best efforts, things go wrong. Fortunately, Scrivener 3 has automatic backup settings. If you are concerned about the frequency of your backup files, you can backup manually by clicking on File ‣ Backup ‣ Backup Now.

Before automatic backing up can occur, you have to set it up in Options (CTRL+). Choose the Backup tab and set up a location and the behavior you want Scrivener to do when backing up. If you don't have issues with hard drive space, I recommend keeping more than just five backup files. If you don't use an external drive to back up your whole hard drive, I suggest you set this location somewhere on the cloud. Personally, I have my backup files saved in a different cloud service than I keep my active documents. I save my works in progress to Dropbox but my backup files on the iCloud.

If the catastrophic happens, first take a deep breath. Then go to Options (CTRL+) and choose the Backup tab. Click on Open Backup Location and a menu of your zipped backups will appear. Choose a backup file that was made before your problem started. Right click on the file and duplicate it.

Drag the copy of your file to your desktop or another file you have created in Windows Explorer. Then click on it. You will find a .scriv file you can open. Although there are other types of files in the folder, the .scriv file is the only one you can open.

Most, if not all, of your words should be in that file. If you are still having difficulties, you might need to go to an earlier backup file.

If your project stops working and you need to restore it from a backup copy, I recommend calling the restored file something different from your original file in case the problem was created by a corrupted file.

You may be saying to yourself, "So, that sounds like a huge hassle. How do I stop my file from being corrupted?"

The most important thing you can do is to wait until your file is completely saved before you close the project in Scrivener.

I know this seems simple, but as your file increases in size, it will take longer to save. Make sure you don't harm your project by being too inpatient.

When you are using cloud services like Dropbox, make sure you have reliable Wi-Fi access.

My next tip may also seem intuitive, but sometimes people forget. Work with your laptop plugged in whenever possible. When your computer shuts down unexpectedly because your battery dies, awful things can happen to your work.

After I lost a substantial number of words because of a computer malfunction, I have become compulsive about creating backup copies. I have my laptop connected to an 8 TB external drive. Twice a year, I backup all of my projects to a thumb drive just for safekeeping. If that were not enough, every day or every other day depending on how much I've written I compile a Microsoft Word document and send it to myself on Facebook. You don't have to be as obsessive as I am about creating backups. After losing fifteen thousand words, it has made me a little paranoid. I need to be clear that Scrivener was not at fault in my data loss, I had a problem with my hard drive which had not been diagnosed.

A corrupt file may not be the only thing you need to troubleshoot. Sometimes, compiling documents can be tricky. Next, we'll talk about some common issues which may create difficulties.

Common Compiling issues

You may have noticed there are a lot of moving parts in Scrivener and sometimes, things go awry.

It can be discouraging when your hard-earned words don't turn out the way you want them to. But if you're having difficulties, I'll give you some tips to help.

Making Sure Your Ducks Are in a Row

In Scrivener 3, there are three areas you need to pay attention to. First, make sure all the documents you want to appear are checked in the compiler. This starts with the very first folder which contains your manuscript. Although it is possible to have more than one manuscript in your Draft Folder, I don't recommend it (unless you are creating an omnibus).

If your Binder contains more than one folder with the same name, it can cause confusion and make it difficult to determine which one you are editing. If you have re-imported your corrected file after you have made corrections in an external program like Microsoft Word, move your old folders to your Research Folder. In fact, it's even better to create a folder called old manuscript and put the files in there.

Make sure you don't have a filter applied. I have personal experience with this, I had inadvertently set this filter to exclude files and then I was puzzled why my whole manuscript didn't compile. So, just keep an eye out to make sure you haven't inadvertently filtered out the files you want.

Next, take a moment to make sure all the documents or files you want in your final document are checked. Not surprisingly, I've also made this mistake. Imagine my humiliation when I discovered such a basic mistake. So, take a simple lesson from me and double check to make sure everything is included in your Compile Pane.

Assigning Section Types to the wrong Section Layout when you assign them in the Section Layout Pane can skew your output. If that happens, just reassign them in the Compiler.

As I talked about earlier, if you are having trouble with your table of contents, make sure you examine the separator settings so that you don't inadvertently use a page break when you intend to use a single line or return. Page breaks trigger entries in your table of contents.

Make sure you are using the correct placeholders when you set up your format options. A single letter can throw off your entire layout.

Text Color and Hyperlinks

Scrivener makes it wonderfully simple to be creative when you write. However, sometimes you may not want to share the extent of your creativity with everyone else. If you are like me and write with your text in a different color, you probably want your text to appear normal in your document when it is output. If so, you can check the box in the compiler to remove text color. This setting returns your text color to black (or white on a dark background).

Using hyperlinks in Scrivener 3 is pretty easy. However, the way you access them is not intuitive. Instead of being on the insert menu, you can find hyperlinks under Edit ▸ Add Link. From here, it acts as a traditional hyperlink tool. To make the link above, I just highlighted the words Scrivener 3 and inserted a hyperlink to their website.

If you right-click on a hyperlink, you can edit it or remove it entirely.

This is a handy feature because when you upload books to other platforms, they do not allow links directly to Amazon.

There may be times when you do not want hyperlinks to appear in your final document. You can have Scrivener remove the hyperlinks in your output by changing the setting under the gear in the Compile Pane.

Issues with Graphic Size

I recently encountered a problem with my format when I started another series and needed a different chapter heading graphic. For whatever reason, my new graphic wasn't displaying the same as my previous one. Once again Bobby Treat came up with a great solution. I want to share it with you in case you encounter the same difficulties.

If you need to adjust the size of your images in Scrivener 3, you can easily do so with placeholders. This is a two-step process. It's really helpful because you can resize your images based on the type of output you are using. For example, your image may look one way at 72 DPI for an e-book but need to be resized when you output them at 300 DPI for your paperback. Scrivener allows you to adjust this easily.

The first step is to add a placeholder to your image in your format. ImageWidth is just a term to identify what we want

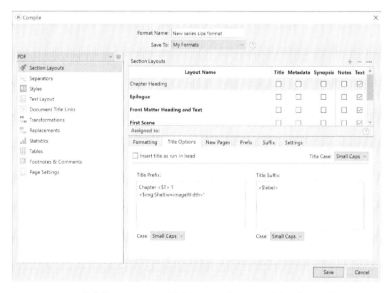

FIGURE 74: Adding ImageWidth as a Placeholder (Part 1)

replaced. You could use any term here. You will need to repeat these steps in every Section Layout in which you have an image you need adjusted.

The next step is to add the definition of ImageWidth into the replacement tool.

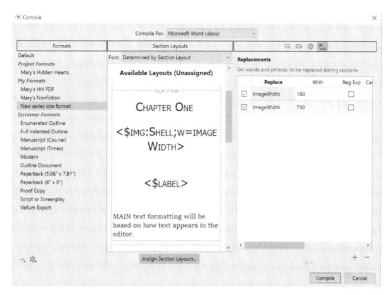

FIGURE 75: Adding Image Width as a Placeholder (Part 2)

In the example above, I defined the ImageWidth as 180 pixels for the e-book and 750 pixels for the paperback. After you've set your ImageWidth, you are ready to compile and create a beautiful book. You may have to play around to see which setting works best for your image. You can easily do this by adding more image widths to this replacement list and trying each one out individually. It works best to only check one box in this window.

If Section Types are not being assigned the way you expect them to be, make sure your folders are in the correct hierarchy in your Binder. If they are indented differently, the Section Type may not be applied properly. (This concept is similar to the levels feature in earlier versions of Scrivener.) It can be found under Project Settings.

Glitchy Formats

I'm not even sure what to call this or even if it needs its own section, however in case your formats suddenly stop working, I want to share with you my workaround or solution. I have encountered one anomaly that I haven't seen reported much. This is why I am so fanatic about backing up all my settings in Scrivener, including my preferences and my formats.

After using a format for quite some time, it can appear to become degraded and leave out sections of your manuscript for no clear reason. I have found that deleting the offending format and importing a fresh copy helps eliminate this issue. Like I said, I'm not a computer programmer, so I'm not sure what is causing this to happen. I just have a practical solution.

As great as Scrivener 3 for Windows is, sometimes you might want to go mobile. So, next I will briefly overview working with Scrivener for iOS.

Working with iOS Scrivener

Many Scrivener fans like to take their work mobile. Fortunately, Scrivener has developed an iOS version of their software. It is not as full featured as the Windows version, but it gives you a way to work with your files in a familiar format and sync them back to your computer. For less than twenty dollars, this is an economical way to add writing tools to your workflow.

After you have purchased and downloaded your app from the Apple Store, the next thing you'll need is a Dropbox account. This is required to work with iOS syncing.

If you want to use the IOS version with your files, the default syncing path looks like this:

Dropbox ▸ apps ▸ Scrivener ▸ [project name]

You can change where Dropbox looks for your files by clicking on the edit button on the upper left-hand side of the app. After you do that, there is a gear down at the bottom left which will allow you to change your settings including your default Dropbox location.

If you have already synced some files to Scrivener from your old file location, the program will ask you if you want to keep those projects or discard them.

If you want to work with your existing files in your iOS version of Scrivener, you need to make sure your projects are copied into the folder on Dropbox where you told Scrivener iOS to look for them. You can do this via the Windows Explorer program.

Make sure you are copying the whole Scrivener project. These will end in .SCRIV. Files that end in .XML are not full Scrivener projects and should not be moved separately.

If you plan to upload your projects to your iPad, make sure you have Wi-Fi access and plenty of time. Scrivener files can be quite large and take quite some time to upload to your iPad. I learned the hard way that you shouldn't try to do this on the road with limited Wi-Fi.

If you have several Scrivener projects, you may want to direct Scrivener to search for your work-in-progress in a file with very few other Scrivener projects. Having fewer projects to sync will help speed up the process. If you are having difficulty syncing your projects with the iOS version, double check your Wi-Fi connection and make sure it is functioning properly.

Most of the features of Scrivener for Windows are available in the iOS version. For example, you have access to the Binder, your Inspector and a Scrivenings window. Additionally, you can work with your corkboard and Index cards as well as your labels and status.

You can also add a new project from scratch. Scrivener iOS allows you to add documents and folders just as the Windows and Mac version do.

If you have changed your project when you go back to the project list, there will be a blue triangle in your project. This symbol shows your project needs to be synced. You can set your iPad or iPhone to automatically sync Dropbox files in the settings or you can use the sync button on your device.

When you go back to your Windows computer you can check to make sure the changes have been synced by clicking on File ▸ Sync ▸ Mobile Devices.

Do not use File ▸ Sync ▸ External Files to sync with iOS. This setting is intended to sync your files to outside files. This does not update your Scrivener iOS file. It is designed to export text files to an external file.

Although there is mixed advice on this topic, I recommend that you save and close your file on your computer before trying to sync it with the iOS device. I have heard contrary advice which suggests that you can have both versions open at the same time. I have not found this to be the case.

To ensure your syncing process goes smoothly, make sure you have good Wi-Fi access and you wait until Dropbox is finished saving your file before you close it. Failure to do so can cause data loss.

 Once you have uploaded your project to Scrivener iOS, you don't need Wi-Fi access to work on your file. You just need Wi-Fi access to sync your files.

If red icons appear on your project in iOS after you have synced it, try syncing it again. Sometimes it can take more than one try.

This was just an overview of working with Scrivener iOS. If you need more help, Literature and Latte has several tutorial videos on their site.

CHAPTER 15

Wrap up and Random Thoughts

I just threw a huge load of information at you. I hope you find it helpful. If your head is reeling, I want to remind you that although Scrivener 3 for Windows is a powerful piece of software, you need not learn all of it at once. You can learn the pieces you use most often and then supplement your knowledge as you go along.

Having said that, one of the best ways to learn Scrivener is just to dive in and experiment. If experimenting is terrifying to you, you can always make a test copy of your work in Windows Explorer and leave the original copy untouched.

Scrivener is a phenomenally powerful program with the ability to do countless things to help you become a better writer. I tried to cover the features I use most often or find potentially helpful. As with everything else, your mileage may vary. Your writing process may look very different from mine and that's okay.

Scrivener 3 for Windows is different than the previous versions. In most cases, I think this is a really good thing. However, it is important to remember that even though it is more similar to Scrivener 3 for Mac, they are not exactly the same. There are things you can do in the Mac version that still don't function correctly or are missing in Scrivener 3 for Windows. Having said that, version 3 for Windows is a comprehensive, powerful piece of software. I hope you enjoy learning about all of its new features.

Some of you may be asking yourself why I didn't cover Scrivener 3 for Mac in this book. I've written *An Everyday Guide to Scrivener 3 for Mac*, which focuses on the Mac platform. I also have written two other books in the Empowering Productivity series which deal with effectively using dictation as an author.

If you have questions or comments, please email me at Mary@MaryCrawfordAuthor.com or find me on the following social networks:

FACEBOOK:
facebook.com/authormarycrawford
WEBSITE:
MaryCrawfordAuthor.com
TWITTER:
twitter.com/MaryCrawfordAut

Acknowledgements

I am blessed to have a great team around me. They went above and beyond.

Kathy F. may never want to volunteer to help me again after sorting through copious amounts of keyboard shortcuts to verify they actually exist.

Kathern W. is game to read anything I write, even when it isn't a mushy romance novel. For that, I am eternally grateful. Thank you for being my constant cheerleader (even when you don't quite understand my plan).

A special thanks to Stephanie from Alt 19 Creative for her formatting work to make my ideas pop off the page. I appreciate your attention to detail.

Put quite simply, Kathy from Covers Unbound takes my plain, disjointed words and makes them beautiful. Her covers are amazing, and she did a masterful job steering me in the right direction when I had no idea what I was doing. It's a pleasure to work with you.

Lisa Lee—my editor extraordinaire. I admire your grit and tenacity to work under difficult circumstances and still cope with anything I throw at you. Thank you for making sense of my ramblings, so other people can learn something.

Nic Gash, thank you so much for going through my work with a fine tooth comb and helping me smooth out the rough parts.

Lacie Redding, thank you for helping to make sure people know I actually write books. Your never-ending support is more helpful than you can imagine.

Thank you to David Lee Martin, Bobby Treat, Gwen Hernandez, and Karen Price for allowing me to join your Scrivener support community and soak up knowledge over the years. You guys have made me better at my job.

I went to give a special shout out to my husband, Leonard Crawford. I can't tell you how much I appreciate your help and support. Your insightful questions and suggestions helped me create a much stronger book. You are a great cheerleader even when I have to do things twice. Thank you for always being in my corner.

To my son, Justin—I am so proud of the man you are becoming. Thank you for taking such great care of me when sometimes I'm too busy to take care of myself. I understand that helping me can sometimes be a pain. Thanks for doing it anyway.

Resources

Retailers and Equipment:

Literature and Latte
literatureandlatte.com
Scrivener is their signature program (although they do make Scapple). It is my go-to writing program. I own three versions of it.

Nuance®
Nuance.com
The software company which develops and supports Dragon® Dictate, Dragon® NaturallySpeaking, and Dragon® Anywhere.

Speech Productivity
speechproductivity.eu
This $25 to $45 add-in program for Dragon® Professional Individual for Windows is everything Dragon® Pad should be but isn't. I'm a huge fan.

KnowBrainer

Knowbrainer.com

A software and adaptive equipment online retailer with comprehensive resources and an active forum and helpful equipment guides.

Blue Mic

bluedesigns.com

The manufacturer of Yeti, Snowball, Raspberry microphones (among others). These are among the best microphones I've ever used for voice recognition software.

Krisp

krisp.ai

This program creates a virtual microphone which screens out and necessary background noise.

Internet Communities:

Scrivener V3

facebook.com/groups/ScrivenerWinV3

This is a relatively new Facebook support group designed to help those using version 3.

Scrivener Users

facebook.com/groups/463927253627424

A very active Facebook group dedicated to users of Scrivener. Beginners and experts both post in this group. It is a great way to get your questions answered.

Scrivener Mac Heads

facebook.com/groups/1745037292432636

A Facebook group dedicated to helping the users of Scrivener 3 for Mac. Unlike the Scrivener users board, this one is focused on Scrivener 3 for Mac.

Dragon® Riders

facebook.com/groups/1648134245442422

This forum, which covers both versions of Dragon® Professional Individual is the most active group on Facebook. There are many participants who are well-versed in both programs and generous with their advice.

Dragon® NaturallySpeaking Users

facebook.com/groups/1648134245442422

This group is also a Facebook group, but it's focus tends to be tailored toward NaturallySpeaking.

Additional Software, Courses and Books:

David Lee Martin

The most helpful Scrivener tutorials I've ever encountered. David also has helpful books.

scrivener-unleashed.teachery.co/scrivener-unleashed

Gwen Hernandez

Helpful Scrivener interactive tutorials and author of Scrivener for Dummies.

gwenhernandez.com/

Karen Price

Helpful Scrivener tutorial on Udemy

udemy.com/course/scrivener-3-full-course-on-how-to-use-scrivener

Grammarly

Grammarly.com

A web-based grammar checking program. They offer both free and paid versions. Aside from Scrivener, this is my favorite place to dictate.

ProWritingAid

prowritingaid.com

A fee-based grammar checking program. You can buy a lifetime subscription. This program works directly with Scrivener.

Tomato One

apps.apple.com/us/app/tomato-one-free-focus-timer

A flexible Pomodoro timer which allows you to set the amount of time you would like to write and the length of time you rest. It tracks the number of Pomodoro sessions you have completed each day.

Focus

Heyfocus.com

A web blocking app for the Mac which allows you to use Pomodoro timers and customize the websites you block.

Focus Me

focusme.com

Focus me is an app designed to block websites and increase your productivity. It is available for both Windows and Mac.

Pacemaker Press

pacemaker.press

One of the ways I stay motivated is to track my progress. My favorite way to do this is with Pacemaker Press. I can track multiple projects and plan out my year.

Romancing the Beat: Story Structure for Romance Novels

gwenhayes.com/books/romancing-the-beat

Gwen Hayes has created one of the most straightforward guides to writing romance novels I've ever seen. Even better, she has a Scrivener template based on the book available on her website.

The 8-Minute Writing Habit for Novelists: Triple Your Writing Speed and Learn Dictation to Produce More Words, Faster by Monica Leonelle

theworldneedsyourbook.com/dictationresources

This book incorporates dictation into an overall strategy of writing faster. Dictation is just one component of a mindset of increasing your productivity.

Sprinting Groups and Other Resources:

Grotto Garden

facebook.com/groups/GrottoGarden

Need a sprinting partner any time, day or night? Not a problem with this friendly group of folks. Just hop on and introduce yourself. The group is large enough that there are usually sprints happening around the clock.

NaNoWriMo

nanowrimo.org

Why not join us for National Novel Writing Month? Not only is it a fun challenge, you'll meet lots of other great writers and find a website chock full of great writing tips and prompts. It's also a great way to practice sprinting and earn discounts on software and editing programs— including Scrivener.

My Write Club

mywriteclub.com

This is a great little motivating sprinting site. I love this site because it is so flexible. You can join a group sprint which is a group of random people. They have twenty-five minute sprints at the top and bottom of every hour. You can race against a group of people. You earn stars along the way for your progress which is incredibly motivating. You can also set up your own private sprint by yourself or with a group of friends. You can track your progress toward your goal.

About the Author

I have been lucky enough to live my own version of a romance novel. I married the guy who kissed me at summer camp. He told me on the night we met that he was going to marry me and be the father of my children.

Eventually, I stopped giggling when he said it, and we've been married for more than thirty years. We have two children. The oldest is a Doctor of Osteopathy. He is across the United States completing his residency, but when he's done, he is going to come back to Oregon and practice Family Medicine. Our youngest son is now tackling high school, where he is an honor student. He is interested in working for the FBI as an evidence technician.

I write full time now. I have published more than thirty books and have several more underway. I volunteer my time to a variety of causes. I have worked as a Civil Rights Attorney and diversity advocate. I spent several years working for various social service agencies before becoming an attorney.

In my spare time, I love to cook, decorate cakes and of course, I obsessively, compulsively read.

I would be honored if you would take a few moments out of your busy day to check out my website, MaryCrawfordAuthor.com.

While you're there, you can sign up for my newsletter and get a free book. I will be announcing my upcoming books and giving sneak peeks as well as sponsoring giveaways and giving you information about other interesting events.

If you have questions or comments, please E-mail me at Mary@MaryCrawfordAuthor.com or find me on the following social networks:

FACEBOOK:
facebook.com/authormarycrawford
WEBSITE:
MaryCrawfordAuthor.com
TWITTER:
twitter.com/MaryCrawfordAut

Books by Mary Crawford

Hidden Beauty Series

Until the Stars Fall from the Sky

So the Heart Can Dance

Joy and Tiers

Love Naturally

Love Seasoned

Love Claimed

If You Knew Me (and other silent musings) (novella)

Jude's Song

The Price of Freedom (novella)

Paths Not Taken

Dreams Change (novella)

Heart Wish (100% charity release)

Tempting Fate

The Letter

The Power of Will

The Heart of Summers

Hidden Hearts Series

Identity of the Heart
Sheltered Hearts
Hearts of Jade
Port in the Storm (novella)
Love is More Than Skin Deep
Tough
Rectify
Pieces (a crossover novel)
Hearts Set Free
Freedom (a crossover novel)
The Long Road to Love (novella)

Hidden Hearts—Protection Unit

Love and Injustice
Out of Thin Air
Soul Scars
Finding Hope

Empowering Productivity

The Power of Dictation
Use Your Voice
An Everyday Guide to Scrivener 3 for Mac
An Everyday Guide to Scrivener 3 for Windows

Other Works

Vision of the Heart
#AmWriting: A Collection of Letters to Benefit The Wayne Foundation

The Power of Dictation
Pro Tips for Authors:
Make Dragon® Work for You

Wish your words could magically appear?
You are not alone.

What if I told you your wish is within reach? Dictation isn't magic, but it can seem like it. However, it can be daunting, overwhelming, and downright confusing. I've been using voice recognition software for thirty years and written over thirty books using both Dragon® Dictate for Mac and various versions of Dragon® NaturallySpeaking. In this updated and expanded version of *The Power of Dictation*, I demystify the world of voice recognition software for you.

- Learn how to choose the right computer, microphone, and software for your needs.
- This book covers the latest releases from Nuance, including Dragon® Professional Individual for Mac 6.0.8 (Dragon® Dictate) and Dragon® Professional Individual 15.3 for Windows (Dragon® NaturallySpeaking), and discusses how they stack up against other alternatives.
- If you are a Mac user, learn how to get the most out of Dragon®
- Dictate without having to use an alternative operating system on your Mac.
- Explore positive ways to make the transition from using your keyboard to using your voice to tell stories.
- Discover how to increase your efficiency and productivity as you dictate.
- Learn how to take your dictation mobile through the use of transcription.
- Unlock the power of dictation and take your writing to a whole new level.

FOR MORE INFORMATION VISIT:
marycrawfordauthor.com/project/the-power-of-dictation/

Use Your Voice
The Art of Storytelling with Dictation

Does using dictation make your
muse run in the other direction?

Voice recognition software is a powerful tool, yet some authors find it challenging to incorporate dictation into their writing style.

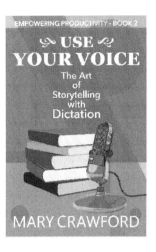

Use Your Voice is a comprehensive how-to-guide designed to help you integrate dictation into your writing process regardless of whether you are a plotter, a pantser, or a planser.

This book will help you choose the software and equipment that best meets your needs. It includes an overview of popular writing software and how those programs interact with dictation software.

Each writing style presents its own unique challenges when supported by dictation. Learn how to effectively incorporate dictation into the writing style which works best for you.

Turn your voice into your most powerful writing tool.

FOR MORE INFORMATION VISIT:
marycrawfordauthor.com/project/use-your-voice/

Empowering Productivity Series

An Everyday Guide to Scrivener 3 for Mac and An Everyday Guide to Scrivener 3 for Windows will be available soon. These guides will help you become familiar with the program and become comfortable—even if you are not a computer programmer.

Index

Made in the USA
Las Vegas, NV
15 August 2022